WOLF

CHARTWELL
BOOKS, INC.

TEXT
ANNE MÉNATORY

HISTORICAL INTRODUCTION
GIANNI GUADALUPI

EDITORIAL DIRECTOR
VALERIA MANFERTO DE FABIANIS

GRAPHIC DESIGN
PATRIZIA BALOCCO LOVISETTI

GRAPHICS
MARIA CUCCHI

C O N T E N T S

1
Wolves are extremely discreet animals that know how to integrate themselves into the environment in which they live. Survival demands no less.

2-3
Golden eyes that may strike fear into one's heart also fascinate: a person captured in a wolf's gaze will never forget those eyes.

4-5
Wolves, highly social animals, need strong relationships to fully develop their personalities. Furthermore, they need to join forces to hunt large-size prey.

6 and 7
The wolf's howl can be a call, an invitation to hunt, a melancholy song, or even the utterance that made it famous as an evil animal in tales like Perrault's Little Red Riding Hood.

© 2004 White Star s.r.l.
Via M. Germano, 10
13100 Vercelli, Italy
www.whitestar.it

This edition published in 2012 by
CHARTWELL BOOKS, INC.
A division of BOOK SALES, INC.
276 Fifth Avenue Suite 206
New York, New York 10001
USA

Translation: Timothy Stroud and Amy Ezrin

ISBN 978-0-7858-2897-6
1 2 3 4 5 6   16 15 14 13 12

Printed in China

PREFACE

It is often said that wolves are 'fascinating' animals. Besides finding them interesting for a number of reasons, I personally have a strong relation with them, a bond that was formed in my childhood.

Enthusiasms are not necessarily passed on from parents to children, but the origin of my interest in wolves was undoubtedly my father, Gérard Ménatory, who dedicated forty years of his life to the study of *Canis lupus*. He followed these splendid predators almost everywhere they were to be found in the wild and got to know those peoples who live in contact with them. He studied *Canis lupus* in huge enclosed areas where they lived in a half-wild state, the only possible way to observe and study certain aspects of their behavior. He was also involved in the process called 'imprinting,' focusing on a young wolf that to all intents and purposes considered him as his parent.

My father's studies were carried out in such a detailed and innovative manner (we are talking of more than forty years ago) that he can be considered a pioneer in the study of wolves' behavior. He was the first to reveal the strength and complexity of the social ties that unite the members of a wolf pack, and he was the first to show that wolves do not attack man. His writings, books and articles aroused strong feelings for wolves in many people. An unequalled naturalist, he was also a protector of birds of prey and of the maintenance, in general, of biodiversity.

In 1985 my father established a park in Sainte-Lucie in Lozère (France) with the aim of understanding wolves better, which at that time were not protected. The park, which encompassed many acres, enabled visitors to approach wolves from Canada, Siberia, Poland and Mongolia and to learn about them.

I worked with my father for many years and when he died in August 1998 I took his place in running the wolf-park. I too have an untiring enthusiasm for wolves and I am always ready to answer the public's questions, to explain and demonstrate. My work requires me to travel, always in contact with nature, and, when it is possible, I hold conferences on the subject of wolves.

In some of my several journeys to East Africa, I have had the chance to study another type of wild dog, the African hunting dog, whose social life is also very complex and comparable to that of wolves. However, my passion for wolves remains stronger and, though I have never gone away for long, each time I encounter one of these wonderful animals my enthusiasm is renewed.

Wolves have always been a part of my life; even my earliest years were marked by this creature: not through stories like that of Little Red Riding Hood, but through contact with their real nature, which is much more interesting than that of the evil creature portrayed to us by the authors of sensational stories.

Since I was very young, I had the opportunity to learn from my father and to follow, even if initially from a distance, the efforts he made to rehabilitate the reputation of wolves and to make them understood as they really are. To him they were animals worthy of the devotion of much of his life, and I have followed in his footsteps. I am pleased by the growing number of people who have learned to appreciate wolves, I think those who still consider them evil and a danger, without even knowing why, are making a serious mistake.

10-11
Hopefully these times will not turn into the twilight of the wolves, in an era that sees them scatter like leaves fallen from the trees, only to disappear as victims of human foolishness.

12-13
Playful wolf cubs mimic future fights: for now it is only a lighthearted game, but the bites will arrive in time.

14-15
All a dominant wolf has to do is show its strength to instantly quell controversy within the pack. In nature, it is necessary to conserve energy.

11

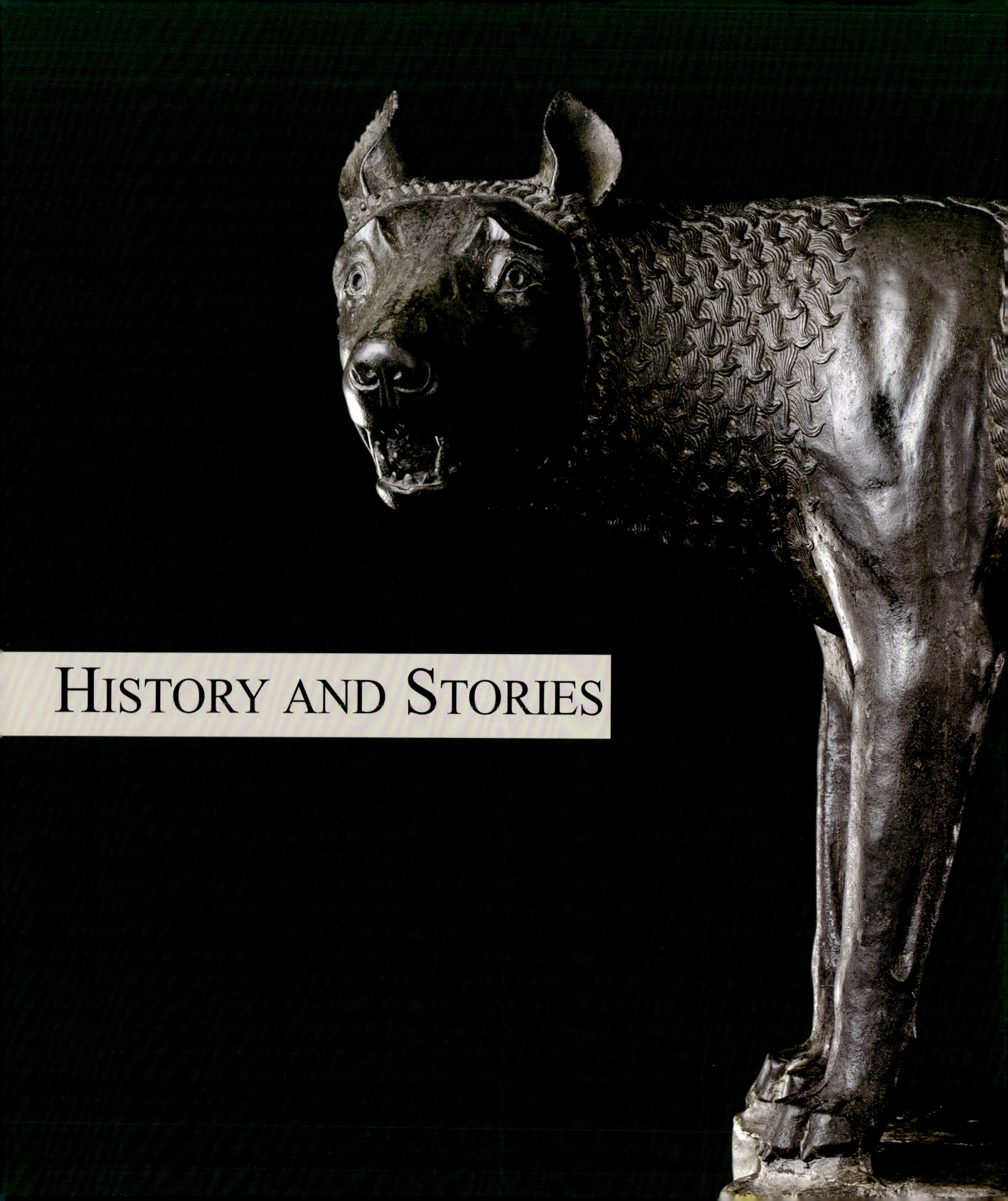

History and Stories

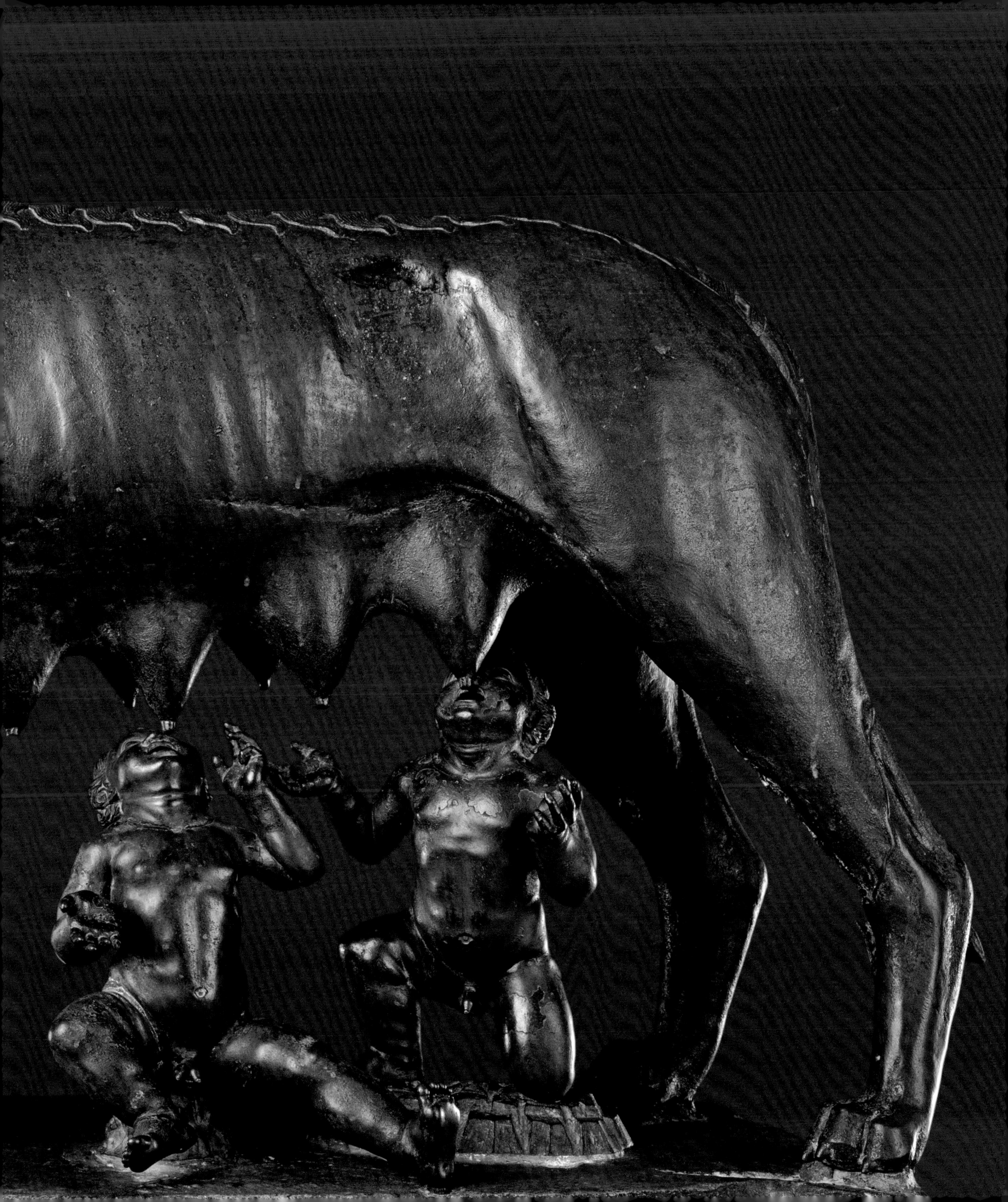

16-17
Romans believed their city owed its existence to the wolf that suckled Romulus and Remus. However, they also thought that to encounter a wolf brought misfortune. This famous bronze sculpture is from the 4th century BC.

18
This 15th-century panel by Sassetta depicts a docile wolf offering a paw to St. Francis. From early times, Christianity assigned a diabolical symbolism to wolves and, conversely, to saints the faculty to rescind this same symbolism.

19
The "big, bad wolf" of the famous fairy tale terrorized Little Red Riding Hood, seen here in an early-20th-century edition of the stories retold by the Brothers Grimm.

A trio of wolves of different origin stands out in the general consciousness of the West: they form a triptych of three panels, the two outer ones filled by the bad wolves, and the central one dedicated to a wild beast that converted to become a good wolf. On the left is the clever but unfortunate Big Bad Wolf from the story of Little Red Riding Hood; on the right the ever frustrated Ezekiel Wolf of Three Little Pigs fame, created by Walt Disney; and in the center, complete with halo, Brother Wolf, the friend of Saint Francis of Assisi.

The first, you will remember, succeeded in tricking Little Red Riding Hood's grandmother and then the little girl herself. He swallowed them both whole but ended up the prey of the Huntsman. The second was a wretched country wolf that never managed to satisfy his hunger with a succulent joint of pork. The Three Little Pigs always get away, some of the time due to the treacherous help of a baby wolf, the son of Ezekiel. The third wolf was maybe the shrewdest of the three: he understood which way the wind was blowing and sided with the Men, like those cowardly cousins of his, the dogs. His adopted an unctuous meekness in the hope of becoming the patron saint of carnivores. But in the hagiography, that place was already taken by a Saint Lupus, a bishop of Troyes, of whom the only savage characteristic was his name. This he used to repel Attila the Hun in his invasion of Gaul as the Huns were superstitious of men who bore the names of wild animals. Like all triptychs, this one too has a predella which illustrates the fourth wolf story we learned in childhood: the Wolf and the Lamb who wished to drink from the same stream, in which the former whiningly accused the latter of muddying the water when he was downstream, poor thing!

Wolves are always notorious, almost always come to a bad end, and have a very bad press. They are disparaged by proverbs and similes: a wolf in sheep's clothing, the wolf may lose his teeth but never his nature, the solitary man becomes wolf's meat, etc.

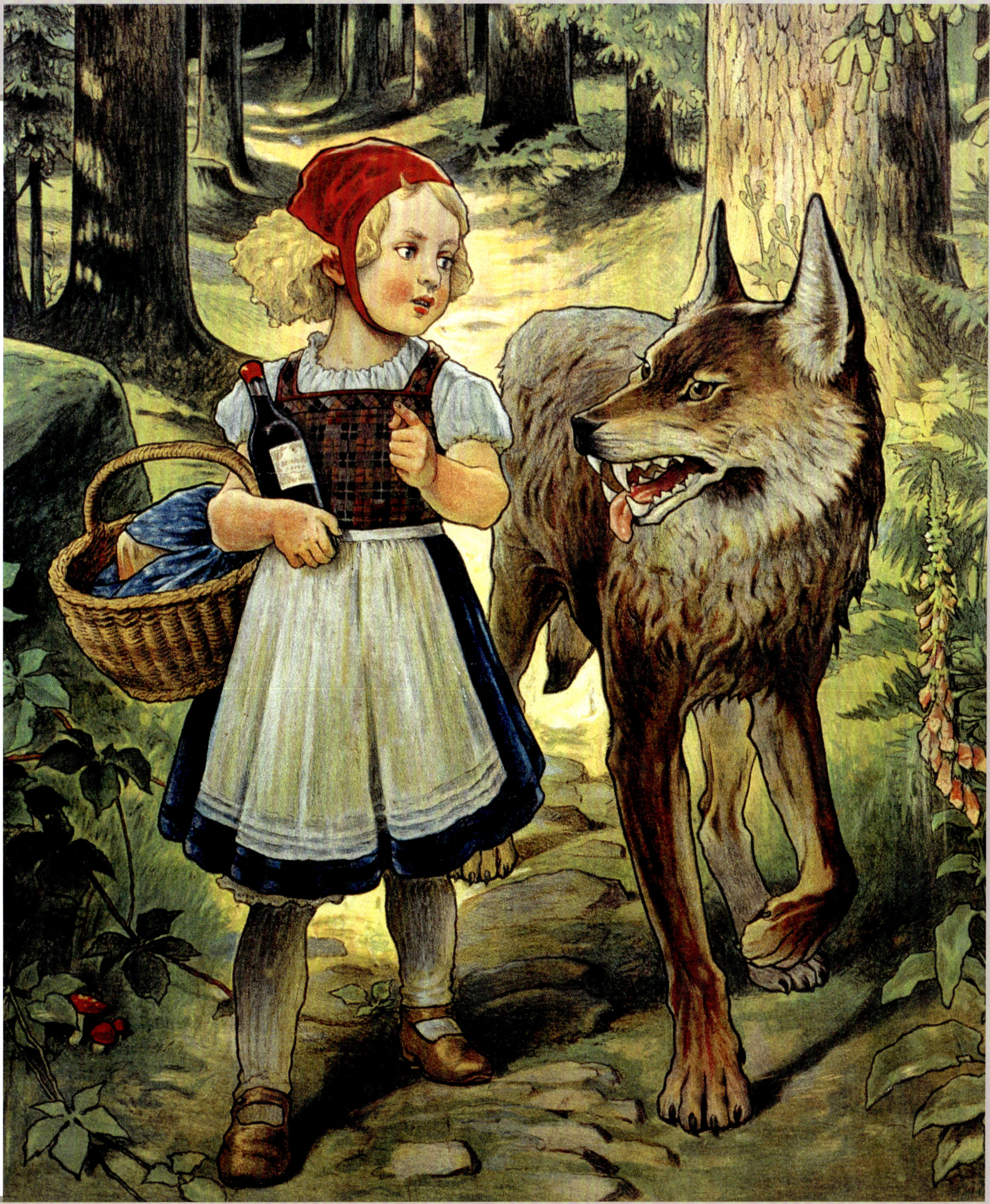

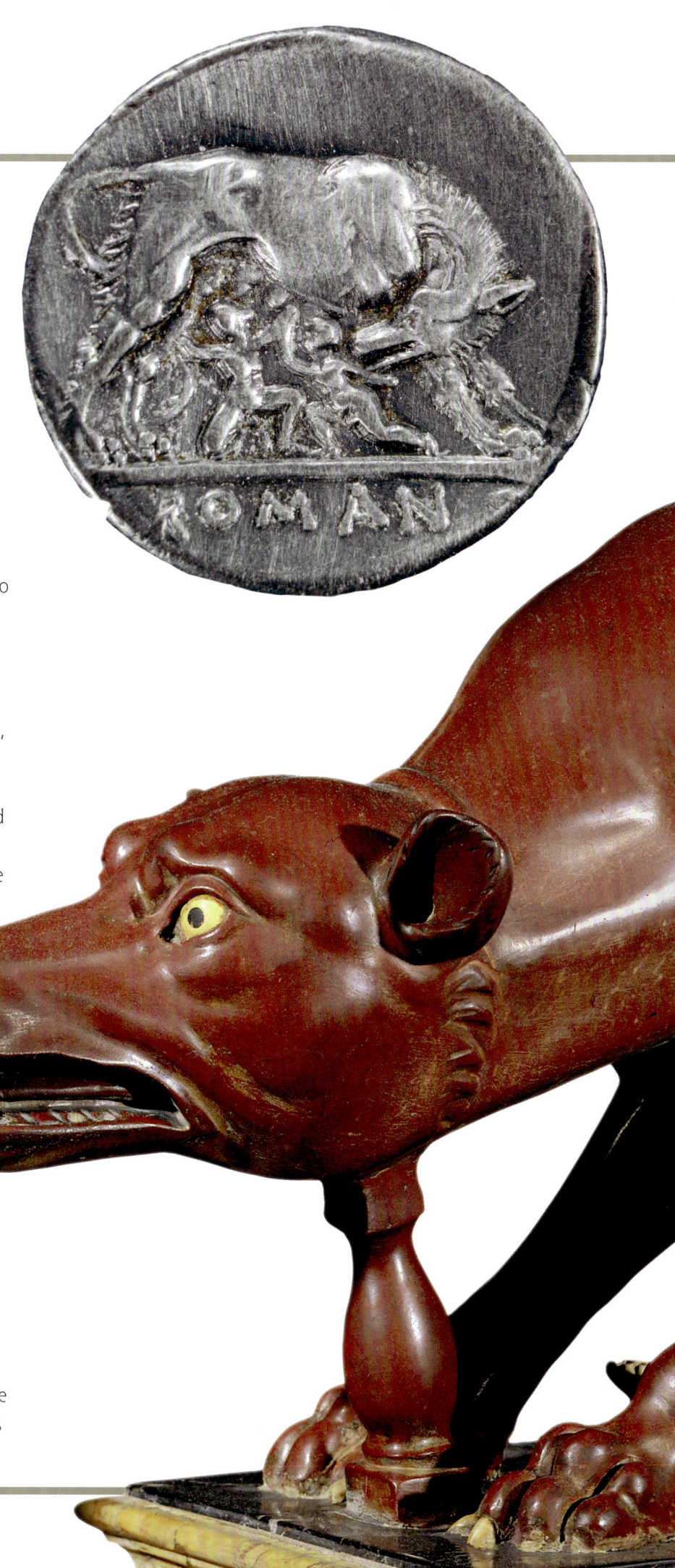

20 top
A 3rd-century BC Roman didrachm shows the mythical saving of the sons of Rea Silvia. The Romans feared wolves, though their apparition during a battle could be interpreted as a sign of Mars, the god of war, and, therefore, of victory.

20-21
A threatening wolf protects the child that represents Rome in this 16th-century interpretation of the myth attributed to Nicolas Cordier. In its powerful role of reinterpreting antiquity, the Renaissance improved the wolf's image, associating the animal with positive characteristics such as caution and shrewdness.

Although the existence of Rome is said to be owed to the charitable wolf who looked after the twins Romulus and Remus abandoned in the river Tiber, Romans considered meeting a wolf in the forest to bode bad things. And they used to celebrate festivities (the Lupercalia) during which the deity Faunus was honored, as he kept wolves far from their flocks. Wolves were a worry to all agricultural-pastoral communities: 'free us from wolves' was one of the most frequently mentioned prayers in the Rigveda of ancient India, whilst in the forests of pagan Lithuania the locals used to request the god Goniglu to keep the 'rapacious wolves' far away. It was only in Delphi – the most important sanctuary in the Hellenic world – that there was a bronze statue dedicated to a wolf near the altar of Apollo. Pausanias, the 2nd century A.D. author of *Journey through Greece*, tells the story. It was erected to commemorate the episode in which the treasure of the god was stolen and the sacrilegious thief had fled with his loot up onto Mount Parnassus to spend the night. Surprised in his sleep, he was eaten by a wolf. Afterwards, the wolf would come down to the city each day and howl as though trying to tell the citizens something, then he would return up the mountain. Finally someone was brave enough to follow and he was taken to where the treasure and the bones of the thief lay. When the treasure was taken back to the sanctuary of Apollo, the wolf was honored by his statue being set beside that of the god.

22

Classical antiquity reported the strangest of the legends relating to wolves, that of the werewolf. Varro, Virgil, Strabo and Pomponius Mela all relate such stories credulously, and later such luminaries as St. Augustine and St. Jerome also believe the phenomenon. On the other hand, Pliny the Elder, in his encyclopedic *Historia Naturalis* (Natural History), forcefully states his skepticism on the matter, despite accepting much more incredible stories quite happily: "We must absolutely believe it untrue that men can transform themselves into wolves and then back to men." This is an example of a 'saying rooted in the people.'

It was said in Arcadia that a member of the Antos family drew the short straw and was taken to a pond. He hung his clothes on an oak and swam across the water, where he wandered through deserts and was changed into a wolf. He remained as a wolf for nine years, living as a member of a pack, during which time he never came across another man. Then he returned to the pond and swam back again whereupon he returned to his former self, though nine years older, and put on what remained of his clothes again.

"It is extraordinary how far the credulity of the Greeks will stretch," commented Pliny acidly. But this comment could easily have included his compatriots, the Romans, as they too firmly believed in werewolves. And naturally this belief was handed on unchanged to the Christian Middle Ages during which demons and witches were principal figures and highly learned theologists and jurists wrote weighty tracts on lycanthropy. The Holy Roman Emperor Sigismund of Luxemburg, who reigned from 1410 to 1437, subjected the question of werewolves to an assembly of learned men who replied unanimously that the transformation of a man into a wolf was a certified fact, adding that any contrary opinion was sinful and heretical.

In 1550, the German scholar Kaspar Peucer claimed in his book *The Northern Peoples* that every December a demon called together the sorcerers in Livonia (a region south of Estonia), threatening to mangle them with blows from an iron bar if they were not punctual. They crossed a river whereupon all the wizards turned into wolves and fanned out across the country, attacking men and beasts. Twelve days later, they recrossed the river and returned to human form. In order to recognize a werewolf, Peucer claimed, you had only to smell their skin because their human skin was simply the wolf hide turned inside out. It seems impossible during that period of wonders that lycanthropes would have the gall to present themselves in a city in full daylight. The Frenchman, Job Fincel, who was equally wise, alleged in his *Book of Marvels* (1556) that a wolf-man had been caught in the streets of Padua. He did not explain how he had been recognized and caged. He declares that once captured the captors cut off his paws – the wolf regained his human appearance, but armless and legless.

In a village in the Auvergne in south-central France, a similar episode occurred in 1588. A nobleman enjoying a little fresh air from his castle window noticed a huntsman of his acquaintance passing by and asked him to bring back some game. The huntsman promised to do so and headed into the woods where a large wolf came running at him. He fired his arquebus but missed and the creature launched himself at the huntsman's throat. The man ably defended himself and managed to cut off a paw with his knife. The wolf ran off howling and the man, seeing that dark was beginning to fall, went to ask for shelter at the nobleman's castle. Asked if he had had any success, the huntsman took the wolf's paw from his game-bag but was astounded to find it was a woman's hand. Furthermore, a gold ring on one of the fingers was recognized by the nobleman as belonging to his wife. He ran straight into his wife's room where he found her sitting by the fire, her right arm hidden beneath her garments. He told her to show him her hand. She informed him that she no longer had it and, understanding that he had married a werewolf, he handed her over to the authorities to be burned at the stake. Monsieur Boguet, who swore the veracity of this story, was an expert: he ended it by commenting that wolf-men couple with female wolves but that wolf-women avoid the attentions of the male wolves. Nonetheless, these monstrous creatures proliferated, for another 16th-century chronicler, Jean Bodin (1520-1596), claimed to have seen one hundred and fifty lycanthropes in a square in Constantinople.

22
A man is transformed into a wild beast and becomes a lykanthropos, a "wolf-man," as shown in this 16th-century Greek manuscript. This legendary ancestral figure has survived powerfully to the modern day, as demonstrated by the belief in "moon sickness" among many primitive cultures.

23
Man or beast? The "monsters" shown here really existed in the 16th century and were exhibited and studied in various European courts. The head of the family, Petrus Gonzalvus of Tenerife (bottom left) had a "normal" wife but their children (a girl, bottom right, and a boy, top right) were both affected by the same glandular disorder.

24 left
A late 14th-century hunting
manual, the Livre de la Chasse
by Gaston de Foix explained how
to catch a wolf – considered a
noble pastime by the aristocracy
of the period. The miniature
reproduced here illustrates a wolf
trap with the bait, an unwitting
sheep, attracting the wolf by
its smell.

24 left
A late 14th-century hunting
manual, the Livre de la Chasse
by Gaston de Foix explained how
to catch a wolf – considered a
noble pastime by the aristocracy
of the period. The miniature
reproduced here illustrates a wolf
trap with the bait, an unwitting
sheep, attracting the wolf by
its smell.

24 right
A pack of hounds and hunters
chase a wolf in the Livre de la
Chasse. Stories of the danger of
wolves and their craving for
human flesh abounded in the
Middle Ages, especially in
France. They were probably true
in part: chronicles tell
of hundreds of victims in just
a few years.

25
A third way to capture wolves
lay in "prendre les loups à la
croupie", i.e., "take wolves with
carcasses." As the illustration
from the Livre de la Chasse
suggests, this method of ambush
allowed more than one animal to
be trapped at the same time.

Anyway, let's leave false wolves on one side as today they are only to be found on cinema screens. Real wolves, on the other hand, have received equally ruthless treatment, though with some justification, because in some regions packs used to inflict serious damage on herds. And during particularly bitter winters, when there was little prey around, they would even attack humans. Medieval chronicles are filled with such episodes, and refer not just to isolated villages, but even to walled cities.

Reading such stories, you can almost see the wolves in action, because they act with such astuteness. Rome during the Dark Ages was largely uninhabited and filled with ruins where wolves used to wait in ambush; it seems it was one of their favorite haunts and a great place for hunting humans. However, not even densely populated cities and towns were safe and in 1427 fourteen people were attacked and killed by wolves just outside the walls of Paris, between Porte Saint-Antoine and Montmartre. Once the wolves had tasted human flesh, they became so gluttonous for it that they no

longer attacked flocks and, in order to eradicate the wolves, military hunts had to be organized.

It seems that France was teeming with wolves, to judge by the fact that there was even a 'Grand Lupatier,' i.e., a wolf Supremo in charge of hunting the animals. Probably they were no more numerous than elsewhere and the impression given of their greater numbers and aggression is due to the fact that there was more written about them. We learn, for example, that in a five-year period during Louis XIII's reign (1610-43), wolves killed almost three hundred people, and that in 1712 Louis XIV sent his Grand Lupatier and his men to the forest of Orléans where wolves had killed a hundred or so people in the space of a few days. And then in 1763 a single furious wolf attacked the city of Verdun and succeeded in killing five people and injuring twelve others before the garrison managed to kill it; and in 1765 the woodsmen in the forest of Sainte-Menehould had to stop work owing to attacks by wolves. They could only restart after a huge hunt had got rid of one hundred and thirty of the creatures.

But the most famous wolf in France, and perhaps the world, was the Horrendous Beast that appeared unexpectedly in the forest of Mercoire in 1764, in Gévaudan – a rugged and wild landscape of rocks, ravines, gullies and thick woods in the heart of the Auvergne. The region boasts a number of place-names related to wolves: Chanteloup, la Table au Loup, la Rose du Loup, the Champ du Loup, le Pra du Loup, le Saut du Loup, and so on. The wolves of the Auvergne are credited with superior cunning: everyone knows the story of the wolf that attacked a horse tied to a stake but was unable to come in for the kill as the horse defended itself so well. So the wolf dipped its tail in a water-trough and sprayed the water into the horse's eyes to blind it momentarily, then went for the jugular. And during the long winter evenings in the hostelries, stories used to be told of the *meneurs de loups* (wolf-leaders), a bland surrogate of werewolves, i.e., men who had made a pact with the devil in return for which they were given the power to command wolves. The *meneurs* would gather together entire packs of wolves and make them dance at night on two paws around large fires lit in the clearings, and then rush off to butcher entire herds.

It was in this setting of wonders and stories that the carnage began. The first victims were shepherd girls who

took the family flocks to pasture, the children of woodsmen taking lunch to their fathers, or who were out collecting wood or berries. In just a few weeks a dozen or so had been torn to pieces. The prints pointed to a huge wolf, but there was something odd: it was summer, when the fields were filled with flocks. Everyone knew that wolves never attacked humans except in winter, when they were driven to it by hunger. In September it was the turn of a woman who was surprised in her vegetable garden, right in the village. Talk began of a huge creature, a monster with a diabolic imagination and abilities. Anyone who saw it in the distance was paralyzed by fear and had difficulty in fleeing. The curate of Aumont, who saw it and got away, described the Beast as 'terribly long,' the size of a one-year-old calf, with reddish fur, a black mane on its back, and pointed ears that were shorter than those of a normal wolf. It swished the air with its thick tail and had rows of pointed fangs that could cut a man's leg in two with a single bite. Naturally hunts were organized which brought down a number of large wolves, but the 'murders' continued. That is what the inhabitants of the Auvergne called them now, convinced that the Beast was not just a hungry wolf that had tasted human flesh, but that it killed for the sheer pleasure of it. Or perhaps it was a divine punishment for the sins of the local community.

26
Peasants, armed men and dogs hunt a werewolf, as shown in this popular 18th-century French print. The theme of the werewolf can be traced back to the moralizing attempt to humanize the wolf, as in this case, or to demonize man by giving him beastly features.

27
The Beast of Gévaudan in this illustration from the London Magazine (18th century) was a rather grotesque animal. The true story of this ferocious animal soon was carried over into the realm of the fantastic; the text here talks of 80 victims, an impossible number for a wolf unless it were possessed by the Devil.

In early October, while the fame of the Beast was being spread right across France by news sheets and storytellers in the markets and country fairs, the hunters of Marvejols finally found themselves confronted by a wolf of exceptional size. The rifles fired. Three times the Beast was struck and three times it fell, but three times it rose again without apparent difficulty. Then it disappeared into the forest. From Versailles, where it was reported that Auvergne was gripped by panic, the good king Louis XV – the Bien Aimé – ordered Gévaudan to be searched by the army. The dragoons of Langogne were the ones to come across the Beast, but once again the devil managed to escape. The bishop of Mende ordered the Holy Sacrament to be displayed in all the churches of the diocese and the prayers of the Forty Hours devotion to be recited to ward off the most frightening calamities. At Christmas the number of wolves killed by huntsmen and soldiers totaled seventy-four, but the invulnerable and invisible Beast continued to strike.

The huge wolf's first setback occurred on 12 January 1765. It had attacked a group of youths who defended themselves with sticks and stones forcefully enough to put it to flight. But then the Beast moved to Cantal where it remained until the spring. But then it returned to Gévaudan to take up where it had left off. Finally, in September 1765, the Grand Lupatier claimed to have killed the Beast in the forest of Chazes. He showed the carcass of a huge wolf with surprisingly long fangs, which he then had stuffed and sent to Versailles for the admiration of the king. The 'murders' stopped – or perhaps not, because in

December, when the snow covered Gévaudan, men and, particularly, women and children were once more attacked and eaten. By 'normal' starving wolves? Or by the invincible Beast incited by the Devil or (another theory) by a 'meneur de loups'? The locals never believed that the Beast was the wolf killed in Chazes, and were convinced that it remained alive even if it lay low. At least in the imagination of the inhabitants, its victims were legion. Considering the story from a wolf's point of view, the Beast of Gévaudan was the glory of France; it avenged the extermination wrought by man on its fellow creatures who were no more than instinctual hunters of sheep and goats. Let's conclude as we started, with a triptych. Placing the Beast in one of the side panels, we can match it with the Steppenwolf on the other, which we can imagine untiringly chasing after a sled that it may never catch on the snowy steppes of Siberia. And in the center, to reconcile the two inimical species, we will talk about the only known example of a wolf-man, or rather a wolf-boy: a child about ten years old who was found in the mid-nineteenth century near Chandpur in India (other two wolf-boys will be discovered in India approximately seventy years later). He had grown as a member of a wolf family, ate only raw meat and behaved completely as though he were a wolf. Taken forcefully into the 'civilized' world, he never adapted, never learned to speak, always refused to wear clothes, and only made friends with a dog. He died just three years later, probably of nostalgia – or a broken heart. The real story of this boy inspired the much happier *The Jungle Book* by Rudyard Kipling.

Beauty, the Beast and the Hero

28-29

Russian art abounds with wolves, as is natural in a land characterized by habitats like the steppes and the taiga. This shiny 20th-century lacquer by Valentin Khodov associates wolves with a figure from the panel, typical of a totemic and heroic theme that goes way back in history in Asia.

29 left

An elegant brocade suit with frogs is worn by the wolf in this preparatory sketch for the costumes for a 1921 production of Tchaikovsky's The Sleeping Beaut. A variation on the theme of Beauty and the Beast, this representation invests the character with a surprising and "dangerous" attractiveness.

29 right
The Tsarevich Ivan rides a
magical gray wolf with his
beloved Elena in this
19th-century watercolor.
In this Russian fable,
the animal is a sort of
beneficent creature that
faithfully serves Ivan in
penitence for having eaten
his horse.

Wolves in fables

30
The wolf "tells his own story" in this series of 19th-century French vignettes. The creature begins to appear less threatening and seems to prefigure the later characters seen in cartoons. The intent is a moralizing one and the tension is discharged in a vivid use of colorism.

31 top
A dog and a wolf confront one another in this illustration from an English edition of Aesop's Fables, published in 1857. Since the 6th century BC, the animals in these fables have been important educational figures in the West.

31 bottom left
Aesop wrote the fable of the Wolf and the Crane, shown here in an early 20th-century illustration. In this case the wolf represents ingratitude and, having been treated well by the crane, has no scruples in eating it.

31 bottom right
The story of the Three Little Pigs seen in a 1910 version by Blanche Fisher Wright. Here the wolf attempts to enter the house of bricks.

TITLE AND DESIGN OWNED BY THE JAMES W. SMITH CIGAR CO.

Tamed wolves

32 top
During the 20th century the myth changed and was adapted to suit the consumer market: the Big Wolf on this cigar box of 1915 associates the animal positively with the concept of "strength," a theme still common for this type of product.

32 bottom
In an illustration from 1880, children at Regent's Park Zoo in London watch a group of wild animals. The wolf is seen on the right. It was common in the 19th-century to exhibit wild beasts in cages as a way to confirm man's superiority.

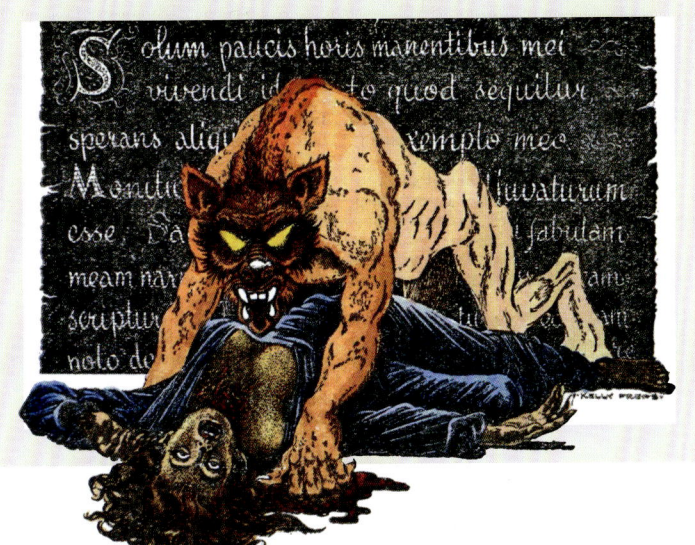

34
The horrifying aspect of the wolf and the hybrid werewolf were reproduced in the 20th century with interesting variations. This unusual pinup of 1938 gives a prevalently (though not entirely) male role to a woman.

35 top
To frighten the public, real wolves were no longer enough. Cartoon strips and popular novels created everyday semi-human wolves. The monster might be the next-door neighbor, as suggested in The Werewolf of Ponkert, published in Weird Tales, 1953.

35 bottom right
Following a custom common among pilots during World War II, the American "Sea Wolf" squadron invested a ravenous wolf with the task of playing down or debunking the idea of war, though conserving the deep significance of insatiable threat represented by the wolf.

Wolves and the fantastic

35 bottom left
The combination of myth, legend, mystery and the attraction of the unusual was illustrated in this 1930 cover, where the wolf is once again a faithful servant of man with superior powers.

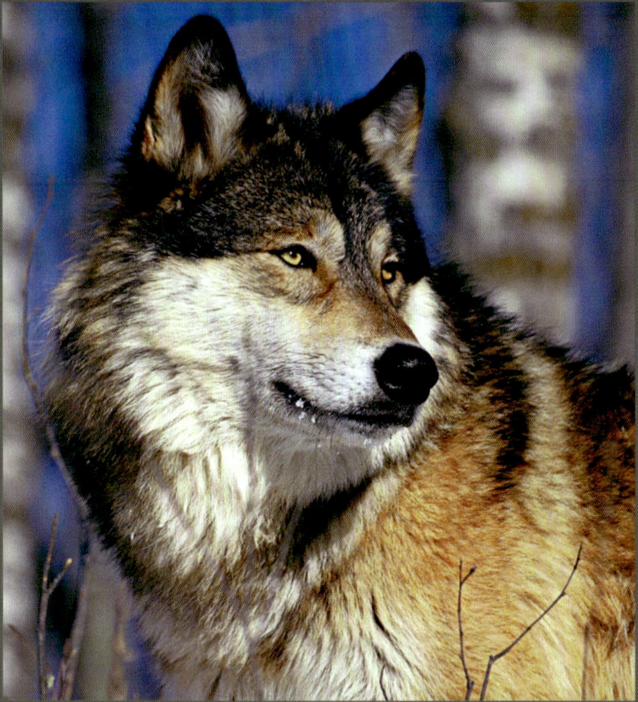
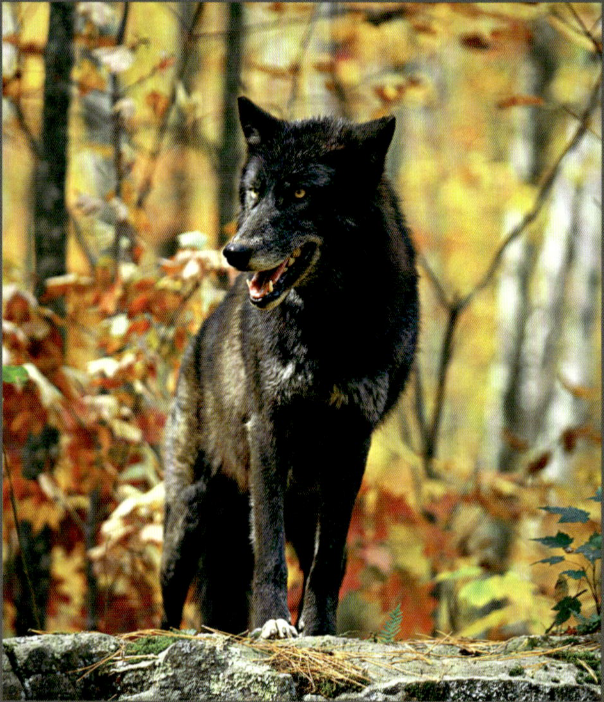

PORTRAIT

36
Wolves of the forest can be gray (or better yet, tawny) or black. Such colorations of the fur, relatively common in North America, make it possible for them to camouflage themselves in the typical environments of their region.

38
Wolves are perfectly capable of surviving frigid and snowy winters. This characteristic makes them highly efficient predators.

39
Powerful animals, wolves can be satisfied with small, or even tiny, prey, which they can take by surprise.

PORTRAIT

With their intriguing gaze, elegant, discreet gait, and noble, independent character, wolves cannot be ignored. This large dog inspires respect for its surprisingly complex social life, its talent as a hunting animal, its capacity for adaptation and its intelligence.

Canis lupus is a carnivore in the super-family of canids (*canidae*), like the dog, jackal, coyote, fox, dingo, etc., and is a member of the class of mammals that numbers about five thousand species. Mammals are hermiothermic vertebrates, have body hair (at least during the embryonic stage) and suckle their young.

The wolf is the largest of the wild canids and is one of the best proportioned: it varies between 3' and 4' 6" in length, and its height at the shoulder ranges from 24"–36." The weight of a male adult averages around 110 lbs and females 20–30 lbs less. The thick, hanging tail measures 12"–24" long and is one of the means used when communicating with body language.

A wolf's neck is muscular to the extent that it seems that the animal's strength is concentrated in this part of the body; as in all mammals, it is made up of seven cervical vertebrae. Agile and quick moving, wolves' shoulder-blades are more oblique than those of other dogs, which allows greater ease of movement. They have a sort of thick, flat mane that stands on end when the animal wishes to appear threatening. With their winter coat, the hairs on the cheeks are particularly thick which, with their slanting eyes, gives them a very particular facial appearance. Their ears are short, but the head is wide and has a volume of about 10 cubic inches as opposed to the 7 cubic inches or so of dogs.

What is most striking about wolves is their magnificent gaze. The amber, yellow or orangy colored eyes of these splendid canids gleam at night in an unusual manner and allow them to see very well in the dark, a major advantage for a predator. The phenomenon is due to a tissue called the *tapetum lucidum* situated in the choroid layer of the eyes between the retina and sclera. The *tapetum* is formed by small silvery plaques and pigmented cells called melanoblasts, which have the ability to migrate along the plaques when light levels are extremely low - or even in the dark. When this happens, the melanoblasts are retracted and the light enters the eye to stimulate the retina, then it is reflected on the plaques of the *tapetum* and excites the visual cells a second time. In normal light conditions, the melanoblasts slide along the plaques of the *tapetum* to avoid overexposure.

The eyes of animals fortunate enough to have this structure (the felids, like lynxes and cats), and which therefore also gleam in the dark, are referred to as 'phosphorescent.' Wolves have a visual field of 100 degrees, but this type of vision is more suited to the perception of movement than of details.

Wolves only kill to survive, feeding on prey that varies with the habitat and season. A wolf can attack a caribou but would also be happy with a muskrat.

40
Wolves have very communicative facial expressions: these help them to avoid fights that could hurt all members of the pack.

41
When a wolf kills really large prey, it dig holes to conceal the food supply. Otherwise, it will stay next to its "booty" for days.

The jaws of a wolf open further than those of a dog (these two members of the canid family are often compared) and are equipped with more powerful 'weapons.' Not incorrectly, wolves are often pictured with enormous teeth, worthy of the bloody and cruel predator that has so excited the imagination and nightmares of generations of children. In particular the canines (called 'fangs') are very striking, much longer and larger than those of any dog. The fangs are used to kill the prey and to chew food. Wolves have forty-two teeth, twenty of which are in the mascella (upper jaw) and twenty-two in the mandible (lower one). Thirty-two of these teeth are lateral and fall out during the fourth month of life, but the first premolars and the middle incisors are already present, therefore, at five months of life a wolf has a complete set of teeth. The set is composed as follows: on each side of the upper jaw there are two molars, four premolars, one canine and three incisors. The lower jaw has two extra molars compared to the upper jaw so that there are twenty-two teeth in total in the mandible.

The power of a wolf's jaws is remarkable: they can exert a pressure of 50 lbs per square inch, and it has been shown that a wolf is able to break the thigh bone of a moose in two. Some years ago a wolf in Gévaudan Park (in the Auvergne, south-central France) lost a fang that measured, complete with its root, 2.5 inches in length. With jaws and fangs of such strength there are few animals it cannot deal with.

Wolves are strong and untiring runners with a powerful neck, wide shoulders and a narrow chest cage. Their fast, effective breathing and long, brawny legs mean that they are marathon runners. They can reach a top speed of 25 mph and, though some of their prey are faster, wolves' endurance works in their favor. They are long- distance runners. The joints of their front legs are turned slightly inwards and their feet have five toes, though one never touches the ground. Their prints resemble those of a large dog but, if you examine one carefully, you will note that the foot is narrower and longer, the heel larger, the claws thicker, the overall shape more regular and the middle toes close together. Important uses of their non-retractable claws are to tear their prey to shreds, to dig the ground and to scratch tree trunks to mark their territory.

Wolves are outstanding in their ability to withstand hunger, pain and cold. Owing to adaptation they can survive at temperatures of 40°F below zero and the worst weather conditions in northern Canada. Their winter coat is thick, and woolly or bristly, which they gradually lose as the temperature rises; in summer their appearance is a little more mangy, indeed, they actually seem thin, however, being muscular creatures, their weight is always greater than their appearance suggests.

The fur is formed from three types of hair present in irregular clumps: long, coarse hair, hairs of different length, and down. Hairs of different type may even grow from the same pore. Wolves shed only once a year, around the end of spring, and in fall the animal's coat completely renews itself.

Wolves do not have long lives. In the wild they live on average for eight or nine years, whereas in a protected area, where their existence is easier and food assured, they may easily reach an age of thirteen. In both cases the average life span is equal for both sexes.

The disparities between the sexes are only the expression of sexual dimorphism and physical differences between individuals.

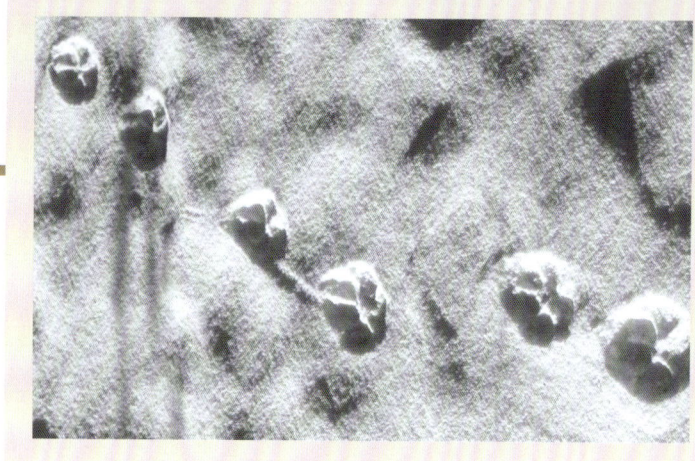

In the snow, wolves generally move in single file, each one walking in the tracks of the one preceding it.

43

In the collective imagination, wolves are always associated with the vast snowbound expanses that represent their most extreme territories.

Females are sometimes more precocious, being able to reach sexual maturity at the age of two, whereas their male counterparts achieve that state a year later.

Wolves are canids and therefore belong to the same family as the dog, which explains the fundamental resemblance between the two mammals, however, there are many differences. There remains a great deal of debate over their origins and this is set to continue: in short, morphologically, the two animals are very close but that does not necessarily mean that the dog is directly descended from the wolf. Consequently the origin of the wolf and dog – two canids with marked similarities – remains highly debated today. Unquestionably dogs have been imprinted by man's requirements, and this is evident in their behavior. Wolves, however, remain independent, even when a cub receives imprinting, and they retain the characteristics of the wild animal. I was only five years old when my father brought home a furiously wriggling ball of fur. The tiny wolf cub was just five days old. She required feeding several times each day and night with a mixture of cow's milk and cod-liver oil. To make her urinate it was necessary to wipe her stomach with a damp sponge. Her eyes were still closed, so her world was formed entirely by smell, providing points of reference that she would never forget. Taïga became part of our lives. When, at ten days old, she opened her eyes, she recognized my father as though he had been both her father and mother. She recognized his smell and the gestures of the person who had fed her and taken care of her: this is the imprinting to which Konrad Lorenz referred, which is so great as to make the animal forget its own species. The result is that the creature only recognizes the human who has taken care of it and who it found when it opened its eyes for the first time. Taïga, a she-wolf from Poland, bubbled over with energy. She had me and my brothers for companions and seemed almost defiant when, at the age of two or three months, she had to sleep alone, a little distant from her 'wet-nurse,' i.e., my father. She howled pensively for a few minutes with a sound that seemed to come from the dawn of time, bringing the shivers to the – hopefully understanding – neighborhood. Taïga grew into a vigorous wolf who, when excited by playing with rowdy children, did not hesitate to cut a chair leg in two with a single snap of her jaws. But a wolf, not even a domesticated one, can be blamed for mistreating the furniture. The experience with Taïga was educational from another behavioral aspect of the wolf. Despite living with animals different from those with which she would normally have grown up with she maintained a certain independence from man. She was unlike a dog, which has need of a leader. We also noted the importance of the environment and saw that the ambivalence between the two sets of behavior – innate and acquired – to an animal 'captured' by man was of particular relevance. For my father these gains in knowledge justified the difficulty of having a wolf in the house, though he would not have recommended it to anyone else.

Obviously little Taïga was not a human, but neither did she become a real wolf from a psychological point of view, and she became scared when she met members of her own species. She received a great deal of love and her presence allowed my father to promote the need to protect the species Canis lupus. All this was very positive, but it would have been better to avoid breaking down the barriers between species, if only because of the

44
When the pack rests, its members frequently let themselves go in a full-on session of corporal gestures, grumbling, and rubbing, all of which are part of a series of behaviors that contribute to clan bonding.

45
The behavior of wolves feeds the aura of mystery surrounding them. Very rarely is it possible to witness any special moments in their lives. This is one of the secrets of their survival.

46-47
Wolves follow and imitate each other: following the tracks made by the leader of the pack. Wolves, like all social animals, need a guide.

psychological aspects. A wolf must live with her own species, not with humans.

We have spoken about the imprinting exercised on a wolf cub, but is it possible for wolves to raise a human child? It is a plausible situation because, as the crypto-zoologist (someone who studies extinct animals) Bernard Heuvelmans says, "The most favorable conditions for a representative of a certain species to be adopted by another species are not parental ties but the biotope and behavior, in other words, their biological niche. From this viewpoint, wolves are by far the animal closest to man." In addition, the highly hierarchical social organization of wolves is very similar to our own. Such an observation may offend those who consider man the superior being, but these people do not know, or do not wish to know, that the human nature of which they are so proud is far from being an innate characteristic. Man, if forced to live alone, quickly returns to being a simple primate. Of the many accounts of the existence of wolf-children, the diary written by the Reverend J. A. L. Singh is the most complete and well documented, and the photographs that accompany it provide irrefutable proof. During a trip in India in 1920, the Reverend Singh, a missionary and director of the orphanage in Midnapore, arrived in a village whose inhabitants told him, "We're scared. At night there are frightening spirits in the wood." It seemed they were talking of a mysterious being, like a sorcerer with human features that walked on four legs. The minister went to the place they indicated where he saw three adult wolves leave a den followed by two cubs and two four-legged creatures with human features. The inhabitants of the village with him refused to approach the den, so the Reverend Singh was obliged to return

later with people from another village who had not heard the talk of spirits. They surrounded the den. Two wolves fled and the third, a female, was killed. At the back of the den they found two cubs and two naked girls clutching one another. One of the children seemed to be seven or eight years old, the other about two. They were both baptized, the elder one Kamala and the youngster Amala. Amala died within a year but Kamala lived until 1929. During the nine years she spent in the orphanage, Kamala's actions and behavior were followed on a daily basis by the Reverend Singh, and described in detail in his diary. It was only in the last three years of her life that the young girl's human behavior predominated over a form of conduct that strangely resembled that of wolves.

Wolves are very attached to their young, and their family ties are solid and long-lasting, the very characteristics that encourage them to raise a human child. But don't we tend too much to anthropomorphize wolves? The mixture of attraction and repulsion we feel for them often causes us to find things that we have in common with them. Today we are beginning to have a more balanced understanding of the animal world as a result of ethology, the science that studies the behavior of species in their natural environment. Modern observation, using sophisticated means and equipment, has allowed us to do justice to the entire species and to discredit the legends that have long influenced common beliefs. We know that Canis lupus is an extremely social creature but ancestral fears die away with difficulty, and anyone who has been 'traumatized' by wolves will continue to view them as man-killers and child-eaters. They do not deserve this reputation of course because in the wild wolves flee from man.

48-49

As the fog enveloping the wolf thins out, people begin to get a glimpse of its true nature. The wolf can only gain from this new situation.

49

Canis lupus knows his territory perfectly since he scouts it without end. A wolf's territory has many strategic observation spots.

50-51
Wolves overcome obstacles with great ease.
They can jump a 7 ft-high obstacle
without slowing down and are able
to take long leaps in order to jump,
for example, from one ice floe
to another.

52
If pursued or simply disturbed, a wolf can
travel up to 60 miles in a single day.

53
Wolves are long-distance runners, but their
maximum velocity is often exaggerated.
In reality, they run at about 28 miles
per hour.

54-55
That wolves are hunters is well known, but if necessary they can become fishermen, even though they are less expert at salmon-catching than bears.

55
The wolf is always on the alert when, as in this instance, it appears to be simply walking alongside a stream.

56-57
A white wolf seems to rise from the snow, a white ghost in a mysterious landscape, an animal perfectly adapted to its environment.

57
Surviving the hardships of winter is always difficult. The support of the group is fundamental: wolves cannot live alone.

58-59
The wolf withstands severe weather conditions remarkably well, thanks to the down layer beneath its coat and its extraordinary resilience.

59
A predator that kills for food, endowed with an extraordinary sense of smell, this animal has all its cards in order to be a perfect tracker.

60-61
A magnificent white wolf in Alaska sniffs
the horns of a cervid – a deer, moose, or elk.
They are probably the leftovers of a kill devoured
long ago.

62

A wolf in the molting season: soon it will have its summer coat. However, to the inexpert eyes, the animal may simply look a bit ill or diseased.

63

The disturbing fixed stare of the wolf gives it, like all wild canines, the ability to see well at night – with or without the full moon....

64-65

Wolves can run vigorously for huge distances. These tireless predators sometimes race alongside their prey for hours in order to bring it down with greater ease.

66
A wolf's display of its teeth is often enough to discourage any intruder or potential adversary. Often this grimace is accompanied by a dry clicking of the jaws.

66-67
The wolf has an extraordinary ability to camouflage itself: with unsettling ease it blends into the landscape through which it moves.

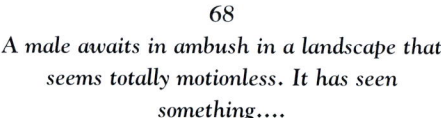

68
A male awaits in ambush in a landscape that seems totally motionless. It has seen something....

69
A wolf projects its greatest splendor when bearing its winter coat, well protected and sure of its own strength.

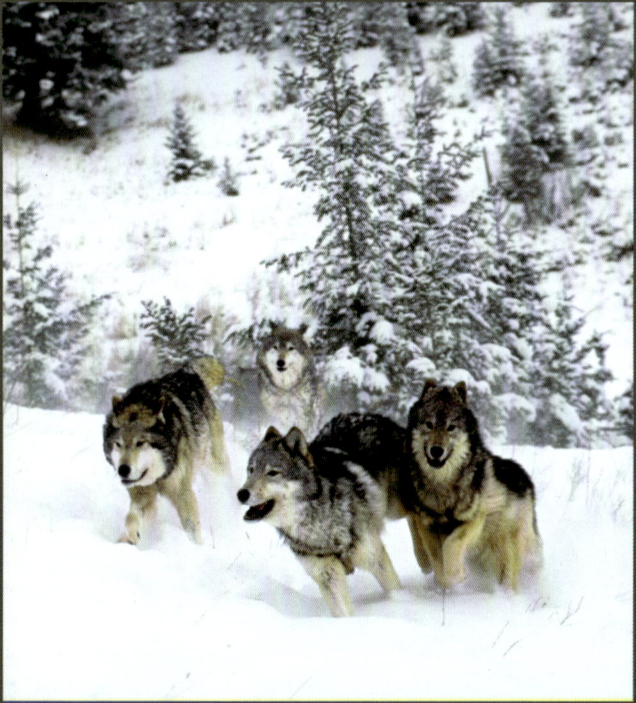

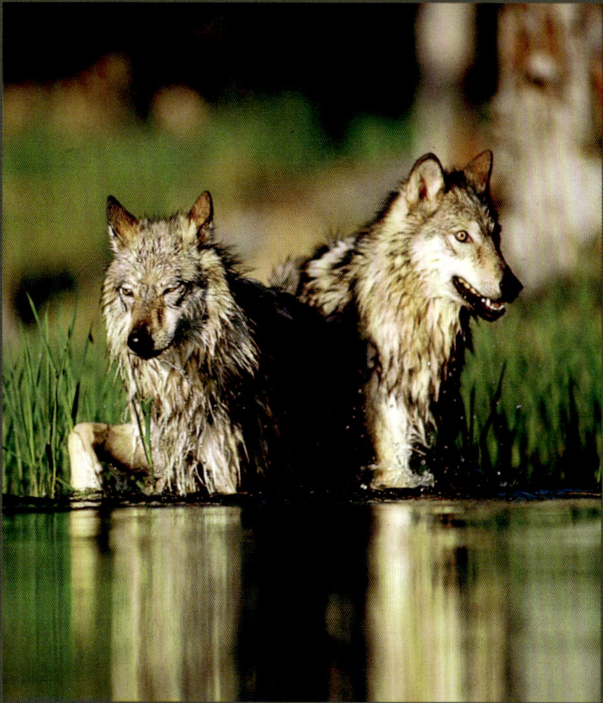

Habitat and Subspecies

70 left
Adult specimens in an
American pack of wolves
range across the Rocky
Mountains: without doubt,
they are on the trail of some
large prey.

70 right
When it is very hot, wolves
love to take a bath. If possible,
they will totally immerse
themselves in a river,
transforming themselves into
excellent swimmers.

72
Like all living beings, wolves
need water. If necessary, they
will make do with snow or
licking ice.

73
In the colorful tundra, a wolf
scrutinizes the horizon. It
seems almost as if it sees
winter arriving with all its
inevitable changes.

HABITAT AND SUBSPECIES

The variety of habitat inhabited by this large canid is enormous: from open countryside to forests, from pack ice to the steppes, and from northern forests to the Arctic. Wolves inhabit conifer forests in temperate regions (with trees that drop their leaves in winter and regrow them in spring) and polar regions. All animals living in the latter have made many adaptations, the most important being their resistance to the cold and the ability to find different foods depending on the season. In winter they suffer huge problems associated with quantity, quality and type of food. In the tundra the vegetation does not grow and is hidden by a thick blanket of snow, so, in Alaska and northern Canada, large herds of reindeer migrate from their summer territories in the tundra to their winter habitat in the conifer forests. The wolves are obliged to follow their movements.

In temperate mountain areas, wolves find game all the year round as the climate is relatively cool for all twelve months, though with marked seasonal differences. When they are still intact, the forests in these regions are the natural habitat of large mammals like bears, pumas, wolves and deer; an example of the latter is the Virginia deer or bighorn.

Life in the northern forests is dominated by the need to survive the long, cold winters. The animals that do not hibernate remain active all winter so require a constant supply of food. Nowadays, wolves only live in the fairly limited regions of ancient territories. In Europe they exist in Spain, Italy, Portugal, Greece, France (since 1991), Poland, former Czechoslovakia, Romania, Bulgaria, former Yugoslavia and Russia; in North America on both sides of the Canada–US border. There are still many in Mongolia and a few in Israel and India, but in most countries they have been exterminated as being harmful.

Fortunately, for some years now things have been changing: though in some countries there is still strong hostility toward wolves, in others a census is being taken of those present. Given that man's attitude is altering following careful studies of wolves in nature, the systematic extermination of these animals is no longer practiced. In Spain, for example, the number of wolves is around 2,000–2,500, in Italy between 4,000–5,000, in Poland there are roughly 1,000, in Mongolia as many as 30,000 and in Russia a good 100,000.

Though the wolf's situation in the world today is no longer critical, its future remains uncertain and difficult. These animals adapt to different biotopes but, regardless of their environment, their behavior and social life remain the same even in different geographical contexts.

In regions where wolves never come into contact with man, they can show themselves to be calmly curious, or at most, perplexed.

A predator adapted to the cold, this Arctic wolf howls across a stretch of snow cloaking western Montana.

Across the world there is only one species of wolf – *Canis lupus* – but there are thirty or so subspecies. Depending on the habitat, their size, legs, plantar pads, color and other aspects vary. Wolves that live in zones covered by snow for many months of the year have a pale or even white coat, small ears to avoid excessive dispersion of body heat, and plantar pads suited to movements on ice and snow. Below is a description of a few of the subspecies to give an idea of the differences that exist between individuals of the same species, depending on their environment.

The Indian wolf (*Canis lupus pallipes*) is small, slim and has a pale coat. It is found in certain regions of India, Turkey, Israel and Iran where it lives in arid or semi-arid grasslands, rarely entering forests. It is a smaller subspecies of the gray wolf; it weighs 40–55 lbs and stands 18–26 inches tall at the shoulder. It bears a strong resemblance to the red wolf of North America both in size and the shape of its skull. In India the wolf is endangered as it is poorly protected as a species. It is thought that roughly 1,500 live in the desert and woodlands of the western sides of India, and in the nature parks and areas considered sacred.

Another very different subspecies is the Arctic wolf (*Canis lupus arctos*), which lives in a decidedly inhospitable environment. It is the only variety with a thick, almost white coat, which it uses as camouflage in the snow and to withstand the extremely low temperatures. Its ears are smaller and more rounded than those of other subspecies and its muzzle is slightly shorter. These features reduce the animal's exposure to the cold, which is essential when having to survive in temperatures as low as minus 58°F and subjected to an incessant wind. Not infrequently specimens of this subspecies weigh over 110 lbs as the greater the mass, the greater is their ability to maintain their body temperature. Arctic wolves live in regions where there is little prey, so they need large hunting territories; in many cases these exceed 1,000 square miles. The result is a very low population density over the 2,300,000 square miles of ice in question. Social cohesion and the transmission of survival techniques are very evident among these wolves.

The Mexican wolf (*Canis lupus baileyi*) is much slimmer than its Arctic equivalent, being on average about 10% smaller than other wolves, weighing only 50–88 lbs, and standing 28–32 inches tall at the shoulder. Its main characteristic is its long mane that emphasizes the bright colors of its coat, which is flecked with gray, brown, black and red on the back, a tawny belly, and ears and paws that are often black. With the exception of the remotest regions of the western Sierra Madre in the north of Mexico, this wolf has almost disappeared, but in the past there were many found in Mexico and the mountainous areas of the southwest United States.

These wolves adapted best to the forests of conifers and oaks that generally grow at an altitude of over 3,300 feet, rather than the deserts as we were generally led to believe. In the mountains there are also white-tailed deer, hares and wapiti (*Cervus canadensis*), all of which are potential prey for the wolf.

76-77
A magnificent exemplar of an
undeniably robust gray wolf:
the strength of its jaws can be
noted, above all demonstrated
by its canine teeth.

In Louisiana, and to a lesser extent in some limited areas of Texas, there remain a few examples of the red wolf (*Canis rufus*), which is another geographical variety that has adapted perfectly to its environment. This animal owes its name to its reddish-brown coat, which distinguishes it from its larger neighbor, the gray wolf.

The red wolf weighs 51–70 lbs and stands 20–32 inches tall at the shoulder. Its ears are larger and closer together than those of subspecies from warm climates and it is light in build with slim legs. It prefers to live in pinewoods, bushy open areas and marshland, where it has developed a particular pose: it stands on its hind legs to see further across the grass and marshes in an attempt to identify even small prey.

Very similar in weight and size to the North American red wolf is the European wolf (*Canis lupus lupus*), which lives in a variety of very different environments, ranging from the Chinese steppes to the Brandenburg region (east of Berlin, Germany), where it has recently returned. It is about 30 inches tall at the shoulder and weighs 77–132 lbs; its coat is variously colored, with shades of gray, black, red, cream and white.

One of the largest wolves is the tundra wolf (*Canis lupus albus*), which varies in height at the shoulder between 28–39 inches, and weighs from 75–140 lbs. This pale colored animal lives in the large plains where mosses, lichens and stunted trees grow. Although it only occupies 50–70% of its past territory, it does not seem that the Eurasian tundra wolf is endangered.

78
The wolf has realized that it is being followed. With a quick glance over its shoulder, it takes off, disappearing into the trees.

79
A black-furred wolf appears to be posing in a northern landscape between a lake and some birch trees.

80-81
A wolf runs through the snow among the pine trees. This extraordinary image of freedom in fact depicts a form of freedom in need of protection.

82-83
Gray wolves watch a torrent in the Rocky Mountains, an environment that presents predators with multiple challenges.

The Arabian wolf (*Canis lupus arabs*) ranges across the Arabian peninsula and in the protected zones on the border of Jordan and Iraq. This is a smaller and slimmer subspecies of *Canis lupus*, weighing on average just 44 lbs and standing 24 inches tall at the shoulder. The coat is very pale to blend in with its surroundings and consists of thin hairs that allow the creature to withstand the desert temperatures. Its large ears (if compared to the northern wolves) allow greater heat exchange and so lower its body temperature. This wolf is nocturnal except in winter, when the daytime temperatures drop.

Populations of wolves also live in flat regions. The original territory of *Canis lupus nubilus* is the flatlands of Minnesota. This is a particularly large animal that weighs 77–110 lbs.

Establishing with any exactness how many wolves live around the planet is difficult but it is estimated that there are about 150,000. Leaving aside attempts at repopulation, which, it must be said, are still rather limited, the populations of *Canis lupus* are affected by strong fluctuation from different causes. An example is in Karelia in the Russian Federation where the exploitation of forests has increased the territories inhabited by elk, and consequently resulted in a rise in the number of wolves. Another important factor in wolf numbers is the climate, as an early or very cold winter will directly or indirectly result in the death of a large proportion of cubs, even as much as 50%.

The geographic distribution of wolves is very large, which signifies that they are not particularly influenced by different biotopes. Colonization of a territory depends more on the presence of potential prey so that, as noted, wolves are willing to live in forests, open areas and inland mountain ranges.

Wolves make their dens in places that are difficult to reach but always close to water courses. If they are not disturbed by man, or if a den is not overly damaged by bad winter weather, the same location may be used for several years.

It seems that, when influenced by man, wolves may alter part of their habits and preferences. In some countries they have adapted to exploit garbage dumps close to villages but they have also begun to be seen in large urban centers and in woods frequented by man (especially in Poland).

Overall, wolves' territories have been considerably diminished. In Europe their distribution has been notably reduced over the last two centuries; however, they are still relatively scattered in Canada, Alaska and the other American states. A large number lives in southern and central Europe and the situation appears stable in Asia. Although the estimated population is around 150,000, it is probable that the true number is slightly higher. The fact that we do not see these animals does not mean that they do not exist! The same situation was true for the golden eagle (*Aquila chrysaetos*), which was thought to be almost extinct in the 1960s; in France it was thought only fifteen or so pairs of this large bird were left when in fact there were at least a hundred.

Fortunately, there are many wolves, and if there are more than the official figure claims, so much the better! Nonetheless, we should remain watchful: the future of this creature is tough and even uncertain in the countries where it has reappeared after an absence of several decades.

84-85
In summer, amidst the lush vegetation of the tundra, wolves are difficult to distinguish. This environment may seem hostile to man but certainly is not so to the wolf.

86-87
The landscape of the Great North looks almost like lunar. Wolves find survival here easy.

88-89
Wolves rarely leave the woods. Within forest areas, they are relatively safe, whether cloaked in autumn colors or not.

89
The wolf's gaze is penetrating; it may have rested on you for an instant just before you became aware of its presence.

90
Canis lupus can sometimes be an acrobat. However, this generally occurs when it needs to get something to munch on.

91
At the beginning of fall, in Minnesota and elsewhere, rivers can become good pantries.

92-93
*Wolves can be tirelessly playful. They go
to take baths just for the fun of it or, more
unpoetically, to cool off in the cold waters
of northern rivers.*

94
*Some would like to throw the wolf into the flames
of hell, but it is certainly better off among the
reddish vegetation of Montana.*

95
*A wolf in ambush, crouched down in the tall
grass. Its forward-pointing ears indicate that it
has seen something.*

96-97
*In the early morning hours, an Ethiopian wolf
sleeps deeply, curled up in a kind of nest.*

97 top
*Even Ethiopian wolves live in packs. Their
habitat is made up of semi-desert areas.*

97 bottom
*Small rodents and even insects are an integral
part of the Ethiopian wolf's menu.*

98-99
An American wolf in Montana: standing stoically still in the snow, this male is in his prime.

100-101
In Montana, the thick blanket of snow favors the wolves whereas it creates problems for their prey, who sink into it because of their weight.

102-103
On a night with a full moon, four wolves race toward their destiny in southwestern Montana.

SOCIAL LIFE

SOCIAL LIFE

104 left
With ears pointed straight up and lips in a snarl, a wolf tries to intimidate its opponent. It is easy to guess which is the dominant one among these Minnesota gray wolves.

104 right
On the brink of spring, the mating season takes the pack by surprise. This gray wolf in the Rocky Mountains expresses his agitation by howling in the golden light of dawn.

106
At the end of winter, the time for games is over. Wolves must now worry about more important issues: on the right, this male welcomes his female in heat.

107
A wolf feigns submission, exchanging licks on the face with his companion. By playing, the members of the pack establish a hierarchy.

106

Wolves are often described as unsociable and solitary creatures but, on the contrary, they are social animals that search out the company of their fellows. They do not like solitude and the individual needs the pack to live well.

Within a wolf pack an extremely complex social order exists that is unquestionably the most evolved social organization in the canid family. The pack's social structure is pyramidal: at the apex is the Alpha pair (the dominant male and his mate), followed by the Beta pair (which aspires to the role of the Alpha pair), then come the clan's adult members in varying degrees of submission, and finally the youngsters.

A pack, made up of individuals with different social positions, is a compact group in which each wolf has a personal role to play. Every so often one hears talk of 'lone wolves' but these do not really exist in the sense that there are social wolves and solitary wolves. Wolves separated from the pack are able to stay in contact with the group by messages sent through urine, excrement, etc., and their reciprocal movements be monitored.

Why do some wolves prefer to remain away from the group? We do not know but it is possible that a wolf that lives in solitude has been chased away from the pack. Some wolves lack certain characteristics that make them become the victims of the others. If a wolf, whether male or female, is chased out of the group, its situation is very difficult.

It is hard to understand the reasons for such a step to be taken. A male may have had a conflict with the dominant male, or even with a female which, enjoying the protection of the pack, exploits every opportunity to bite her antagonist, forcing him to leave. During a famine, it might happen that certain members of the clan attack those of lower rank to the point that the latter are chased away, however, those rejected individuals, if they are diplomatic or wily enough, can also be readmitted.

Older animals sometimes have difficulty in keeping up with the pack during the chase of a large prey. When this occurs, they wait a few miles away and when the pack has eaten its fill, they arrive to eat the remains. This is a hard law of wolves' social life.

Nevertheless, in general wolves are very sociable animals. Their hierarchical relations are respected but that does not prevent a submissive individual from trying to win itself a higher position in the pack. The order in the pyramid is never static and an individual in a high position may well slip down the ranks, particularly during the breeding season.

The dominant male is 'obeyed' and his authority and decisions are generally respected. The better he is as a leader, the more his relations with the individuals in the pack will be friendly and serene.

The power of the pack's leader lies more in his decisiveness and self-assurance than his physical strength. When two wolves meet, the dominant one assumes an aggressive attitude, standing still, his ears pricked, mane raised, tail high and legs straight. The wolf of lower rank will advance with his ears lowered, tail between his legs and then crouch; he will then lick the muzzle of the leader as a sign of submission and, if the dominant one retains his position of superiority, will lie on his back, urinate and display his genitals.

108
*Two Montana gray wolves play
by throwing themselves at each
other on the white snow, thus
demonstrating their friendship
and the pack's unity.*

109
*Two playful specimens have
fun by running around and
leaping in a sort of ritualized
combat that communicates all
of their competitive spirit.*

The dominant female has an important role in the pack and authority over the other females. Her position as female leader is given by her strong character and her role of reproducer in the clan. The females' hierarchy is usually more direct and aggressive than that of the males.

If members of a pack have been separated for a while, they will demonstrate joy on meeting again by licking one another and jumping on one another. Several times a day, and even over the period of an hour, resting wolves will get up suddenly, go over to their companions, lick one another's face, play for a few instants, then return to lie down again. It seems they need to display their friendship, and it is at moments like these that we understand how important life in society is to them. A solitary wolf certainly suffers.

Play is an important feature in the development of all evolved mammals (man, wolves, etc.), and for wolves is a means of creating cohesion and the reciprocal recognition of social rank in the clan. They are very playful creatures that like to fight over a bone or stick, and will rush off to hide it with evident joy.

Playing, chasing and running are part of their daily life. They run like crazy, throw themselves on top of one another, playfully threaten each other and make use of the posture that is an invitation to play between dogs, i.e., head close to the ground and rear end raised. Play also reveals rank, for example, when a potentially dominant wolf bares its fangs as a sign of intimidation.

Wolves are diurnal or nocturnal depending on the season, the quantity of food available and other factors. They live in pairs, families or packs. In summer they are active at night and head off for the hunt at dusk. It is probably the higher daytime temperature that prompts them to be active at night. They rest during the day when they search out shade or dig down to find cool earth to lie in.

In winter they are active both by day and night and only take short breaks before setting off once more for the hunt; during the mating season too they are very active and rest little.

Wolves are fairly sedentary creatures and they defend their territory, especially during the breeding season. When the cubs are grown, a pack may expand its area of action or even abandon it to search for a more abundant supply of food. When this occurs, it is the leader of the pack that makes the decision and chooses the zone, but each member of the clan has its own personality and its qualities are made use of.

The number of wolves in a pack varies. In Alaska groups of 20–21 have been observed, while in Isle Royale National Park one of 15–20 has been sighted. David Mech, a world expert on wolves, followed this last group for several weeks, which at the time was composed of 15 or 16 wolves. The size of the pack varies considerably as a function of the prey available.

A clan is formed of adults and their cubs or may simply be the result of the casual aggregation of independent animals, however, a large pack is the result of the birth of lots of cubs or the entry of extraneous animals to the group. During a hunt a large group has to act with great effectiveness and efficiency.

110
Unity is strength and the group is the only true source of safety: in the desolate loneliness of Canada, the members of the pack proceed in single file, each one walking in the tracks of the others.

111
The wolf's intense social life is manifested through a sophisticated communication system, in which games play a fundamental role.

The size of a pack is governed by two social factors. Wolves are naturally disposed to create ties of affection, and this leads to an increase in the size of the group, perhaps larger than is necessary for hunting. In contrast, competition for food, mating, the role of the dominant male and competition within the social scale are all factors capable of influencing the harmony, and consequently the effectiveness, of the group. If these factors, due to too many wolves in the pack, produce a negative influence, some members will find themselves forced to fight for their survival. In short, social competition regulates the number of members of a pack to ensure that each has sufficient food to eat.

Another factor related to group size is that the dominant male exercises greater authority over a smaller number of individuals. His role is decisive in the hunt, as well as in the stability of social relations in the pack. There are two aspects to his position: privilege and control. The Alpha male controls the hunt and reproduction, he influences his companions and directs their behavior.

When the pack is at rest, if he detects danger, he will immediately wake the others and keep them on the alert. The whole pack then closes around him, licking his face and wagging their tails as a sign of respect and satisfaction at being part of the clan. They may give off gentle whines that develop into choral howling.

Friendship between wolves is very strong and it is easy to recognize a sort of complicity in certain forms of behavior. Wolves need constant contact with their fellows – a relationship that is indispensable to the survival of many species – and will communicate amongst themselves when searching for food, trying to win a partner, feeding the young, etc. Only

cooperation allows canids to catch and kill prey that is larger than themselves. All these factors explain why such strong bonds exist between the members of a pack.

When the pack is on the move, usually at the trot, it leaves a single set of prints because they move in single file, each one in the prints of the animal in front. They move quickly when they are following a prey or when they are frightened or followed; when this occurs their prints are larger and deeper than when at the trot.

A certain solidarity exists between the members of a clan but the survival of the group is more important than the survival of the individual. When there is no longer small prey available in their territory and the pack sets out on a hunt that may last several days, it often occurs that the weakest get left behind. The others will not wait for them as the health of the group counts for more than that of the individual. If strong wolves waited around for the weak to catch up, the prey would get away and the whole pack risk dying of hunger.

Behavior is an indispensable part of wolves' activities and way of life. Instinct plays a fundamental role but their behavior is very much a result of experience. They have an extraordinary ability to adapt to new circumstances, and this is indicative of great intelligence. They have realized that the life of the group offers greater possibilities of survival.

Socialization begins soon after birth when tiny signals from the mother to her cubs encourage suckling. It continues in play when cubs learn to interpret the behavior of the adults.

Fundamental elements of behavior in the life of the group are indispensable for wolves' successful social life.

112
Wolves are strictly monogamous, and the couples, who pair up at a young age, remain together for their whole lives. Fidelity is the basic element of every union, a rare thing among animals.

113
These two young specimens of the Montana white wolf, about one year old, look as if they are teasing each other, muzzle to muzzle.

MATING AND REPRODUCTION

The most important factors in nature that govern the size of population are the quantity of food available and the facility with which it is gathered. During periods when food is not available in sufficient quantities, the population will decrease.

It is interesting to know the proportion between male and female wolves. For those packs that live in semi-freedom, the ratio can be determined simply through observation of the adults, or, even more simply, by watching the young shortly after birth or during their infancy.

Estimation of the male-to-female proportion for wolves that live in the wild, however, has to be based on the number of animals killed. Many studies have been carried out in different countries and, in most, the proportions of the two sexes have almost been equal.

Within a park, the wolves regulate the births to suit the space available and the number of members in the pack so that they will all eat regularly. The result is that reproduction is limited in the group to one litter a year for each clan. There is, in fact, only one pair – the dominant one – that reproduces.

Male wolves are shy when it comes to mating and prefer to let the females take the initiative. Wolves are monogamous all their lives, and the idea of a 'couple' is a reality for these animals. At the age of one or two, the males and females pair off in a relationship that, without too much danger of anthropomorphism,

might be termed 'getting engaged.' They play together, lie side by side and create ties. If the male is the dominant member of the pair, they may reproduce, otherwise they remain together but their relationship is 'platonic.'

Wolves are faithful and the pairs remain together until one of them dies. This loyalty helps to control the number of births as, if the dominant male were to mate with all the females in the pack, after a short period the population would be much too great.

At the start a clan is composed of a male, a female and their young, but when cubs are born two or three individuals will join the group. This is to help raise the cubs as well as to bring new blood into the family group. Blood relationships are almost non-existent and the mating of parents with children or between siblings is extremely rare.

Sometimes wolves of two years of age will leave the clan to search for a partner or a pair may leave to form their own pack, but as the pack represents security, not all wolves have the courage to leave. The various arrivals and departures bring new blood and are a means of maintaining the species healthy.

The mating season begins around February but a month earlier the male wolves use play as a means to test their strength against potential rivals.

At the end of winter, over about three weeks, the females are in heat, the males stop playing and the leader of the pack imposes his dominance through furious battles.

114
The male comes up next to his companion in heat and smells her: the female canis lupus goes into heat only once a year, as opposed to other canines.

Procreation by the dominant pair is an infallible method for regulating the number of births and avoiding the risk of overpopulation, a phenomenon that would harm the survival of the pack. The Alpha pair is usually the one that produces the strongest cubs, and this, in itself, is a further way for the species to be given the greatest chance of survival.

The position of the pack leader is contested every year through fierce fights. He may remain in his dominant position for two or three years but when he begins to grow old his strength ebbs and a younger rival will replace him. The longer a wolf remains the leader, the more traumatic the loss of his status will be. A leader who loses his place takes a hard knock, often ages rapidly and may even prefer to withdraw from the collective life of the pack.

Mating is an important event in the life of wolves. It takes place each year in the same period, with the same behavior and rituals. At first the males are timid and it is the females that provoke them using different behavioral gestures; for example, they may tap their paws against the males' faces or necks or even mount them and simulate mating. Such gestures may occur several times in a day over a period of several days. The excitement generated within the pack will stimulate young pairs to copy the behavior, and the result of this is that the social roles within the pack become subject to change. Sometimes this period of the year is the occasion for lower-ranking individuals to demonstrate surprising daring. It is only the cubs up to about nine months of age that are not involved in this adult behavior.

All the adults attempt to improve their position within the hierarchy during this season and repercussions on the future of each pack member are at stake.

Very interesting social behavior takes place in February. Communication between pack members reaches its highest point, with howls, whines, snarls and body language. All postures are exaggerated – aggressiveness, fear, boldness and submission – and the general behavior is exacerbated by an almost permanent state of excitement. As the wolves are almost constantly on the alert, they sleep and eat less.

I have seen a certain disquiet related to mating appear in a pack in January but attempts to mate were unsuccessful. It was only a few weeks later, in late February and early March, that the mating became reproductive, and sixty-three days later the female gave birth. I have also seen Alpha males (the dominant ones) not simply behave so that lower-ranking males were kept in their place, but actually kill them. Such rare events seem to be preventive in nature, as though the dominant male was acting to preclude problems arising during the mating period itself.

Alpha females also keep a close eye on their female underlings and will warn them by growling if they think the lower-ranking females are approaching a male with mating intentions. They may even kill overly determined rivals. Fights may be repeated every day and a male that has been taught a lesson may prefer to stay away from the others for a short while. Lower-ranking males, i.e., those that have come off worst in a fight or which have preferred to submit without a fight, do not mate. They suffer a condition of stress and inhibition that has been referred to as 'psychological castration.'

115 *Male wolves mate like dogs, mounting the back of the female, which does not mature particularly early, reaching sexual maturity only when about two or three years old.*

The females suffer an analogous phenomenon, and some are so afraid of the Alpha female that they do not even go on heat. The power that the dominant members have over the rest of the pack is clear.

During the mating of the 'chosen' pair, the pack experiences great agitation. Grouped around the pair, the other members take advantage of the moment to bite and attack them. Coupling occurs in the same way for wolves as it does for dogs and all other canids: the male approaches the female and mounts from behind. The erection of the penis begins from the gland at the base and continues after penetration of the vagina. The swollen tip of the penis is engorged by the dorsal artery and completely fills the vagina until it is unable to move. At this stage, the first phase of coitus has been concluded. Now the male climbs down off the female and turns to face in the other direction, raising one rear paw over the penis, which remains inserted in the female. The two animals are now facing in opposite directions; this is possible because the base of the penis flexes and twists as the males climbs off the female though the swollen tip remains in the vagina.

The second phase may last for up to twenty minutes, during which time the penis remains in place and ejaculation occurs. The sperm is rich in spermatozoa at the start of coition but is slowly impoverished until they have all been ejaculated into the female (an average-sized wolf produces roughly 1.2 cubic inches of sperm). The semen does not coagulate because it contains a fibrinogenous agent that neutralizes the coagulating power of the blood plasma. The penis then deflates and the pair separate.

Life in the pack returns to its normal state. The pack accepts its defeat and recognizes the authority of the Alpha couple. The superiority of the dominant female is asserted and the other females approach her with their tails between their legs and ears flattened. They recognize her dominance by licking her jaws as a sign of gratitude for being the mother of the cubs that will ensure the future of the pack. It is rare to see two pregnant females in the same pack, but, if it should happen, usually the 'supplementary' litter will not survive.

Another factor that regulates the number of wolves is the relatively late age – not younger than two years – that females reach sexual maturity. The same holds true for males, which remain immature until they approach three, but often they are too inexpert to win the right to mate and are therefore obliged to cede their place to older and more capable males.

Physical strength is not enough to win a dominant role. A large male may be stronger than the other males in the group but will not necessarily become the leader, whereas a smaller male may win the position due to strength of character and experience. Even among females, determination is more important than physical strength.

Behavioral maturity is as important as sexual maturity. It sometimes happens that some wolves never reproduce but these individuals establish their niche by, for instance, looking after the cubs or playing role essential to the survival of the pack. The complex social life and natural factors ensure that overpopulation does not occur among wolves. A peculiar element is the faithfulness of the pairs, which is very rare in the animal world and almost unknown among other canids.

116-117 Bonds within the pack are extraordinarily strong, above all between couples, as this image suggests evoking a feeling almost of tenderness.

In Gévaudan Park, where the wolves live in semi-freedom, I observed the behavior of a three-year-old Siberian wolf who had lost his mate during a violent fight between packs. For more than a month the wolf remained separate from the group and howled all day long in a sad manner to which no response was given by the others. He was probably suffering the loss of his companion. He no longer played with his fellows and voluntarily remained isolated. The other members of the pack did not ignore him but they left him in peace, with apparent respect for his feelings. After a few weeks, the unhappy animal returned to the life of the group, reacquired his role and, a few months later, found himself a new companion. Later he became the dominant male and held the position for a long time.

Wolves are faithful but, clearly, if they are 'widowed' they suffer from the event. It may also happen that a male forgets his obligations as a member of a pair and has two females, or that a female betrays her partner, but both events are very rare. Social ties are very strong and are reinforced by mating. The physiological act of coupling creates a bond that unites a pair for a very much longer period, often for their whole lives. It is possible that copulation helps to strengthen a pair's mutual commitment, which begins with intimate contact during the mating season. Perhaps the more contacts that are experienced during this period tend to protract those contacts which are more detached in the other pairing situations. The relations between wolves are difficult to understand, and it is almost impossible to establish with certainty what the underlying factors of friendship or enmity are. Their social bonds are created or strengthened during the breeding season, which takes place in spring after a gestation period of two months duration.

118

The wolf howling at the moon is not just a stereotype but an indication of wolves' great ability to establish efficient communication between members of the clan.

119

This wolf seems to want to grab the attention of its pack for something important. However, its howl could just simply be an invitation to play or share a lazy moment.

COMMUNICATION

Communication is a fundamental aspect of life in the pack. Wolves are evolved animals with a complex social life and a sophisticated form of communication. The most easily recognized means of communication is the howl. Is there anyone who has not seen at least once a photograph of a wolf howling at the full moon? This is a highly communicative form of expression. When a wolf howls, regardless of the situation, whether standing, sitting or lying down, the entire pack joins in, including the cubs. It is used to mark the bounds of their territory, to localize ('place') one another, and to reinforce the cohesion between members of the pack; however, it can also be an invitation to play, to hunt or simply a relaxed and composed message. On the other hand, howling can also herald a squabble within the group or with another clan.

Wolves can communicate over a distance of up to five miles using a wide variety of sounds and they make use of a series of signals to mark the boundaries of their territory; in this sense, their howls form a sort of sonic frontier. Howling rarely lasts more than ten minutes and is transmitted at a frequency of between 150 and 780 cycles per second. Sonogram analyses show that more than twelve harmonics, i.e., different tonalities, exist in a wolf's howl. It is also the most effective and characteristic of the five types of sonic communication used by wolves, the others being a whine, growl, short bark and squeak. A human can hear a howl up to five miles away but the hearing of wolves is much more acute.

When moving at night or during hunts, this form of communication allows isolated individuals to rejoin the group. Cohesion of the pack and the survival of isolated individuals would both be badly compromised if wolves, which range over large territories, had to rely on only their sight and smell. In addition to localizing the group or aiding in catching prey, howls can be used to exteriorize sensations or feelings that we can only guess at – but let's leave that mystery to the wolves, as it makes them more interesting! A wolf and its particular howl cannot be dissociated. This form is their most expressive means of communication and, however much it has been associated with the concept of death, filling generations of humans with fear, in reality it is a melodious song and the symbol of a celebrated animal. Observations by American researchers, by my father for over forty years and my own prolonged research in the field show that the howls of wolves vary in the same way that the voices of humans vary when they sing. There are differences in the register, intensity and duration of the sound, and each howl has its own distinct characteristics, like the timbre of a voice. Furthermore, the various harmonics that complement the basic sound give the howl of each wolf a personal quality. We can deduce therefore that wolves are perfectly aware of the differences in sound that they emit and hear, in addition to the fact that they have a repertoire of personal howls for different occasions. Also that they are able to recognize one another by their howls and would therefore be able to tell if a particular howl came from a known individual or from a wolf from outside the pack. Certain sounds, like the pealing of bells or a siren, can set wolves off howling, and it is not uncommon for dogs to bark or howl at the sound of a siren.

120
A group of adult gray wolves acts out some of their most typical playful behaviors within the pack's system of communication.

121
Two specimens of the European wolf confront each other: the dominant one takes on an aggressive stance, with its ears pointed straight up and its paws planted firmly.

During the mating season, usually during February, wolves howl more often as a result of a pressing need to communicate at a moment of great importance to the life of the pack. It is an intense period on which the survival of the species is at stake. In April and May, however, the frequency of howling falls off as the instinct to protect the den and young is stronger. As the cubs represent the survival of the species, they receive all the pack's attention.

The life of the pack consists of games, hunts, disputes, periods of calm and, at times, fights. They play in silence. As they are discreet animals, the absence of sound represents a form of security and is indispensable during the hunt because being able to approach prey in silence is obviously an advantage. Consequently, during a hunt wolves communicate only through body language.

Yet in certain circumstances wolves are very noisy, in particular when they are quarrelling over the hierarchic roles within the pack. Muted growling constitutes a warning, while a threatening snarl accompanied by the clicking together of the jaws can rapidly degenerate into a bite. A short bark is a mixture of provocation and fear. Whines can either be manifestations of pleasure when members of the pack are happy to meet, or gentle communications to the cubs when, for example, the adults wish to feed them; on occasion whines follow on from a squeak or are the prelude to a howl.

Other communications are sent in the smells of excrement or urine, the latter of which has a personal odor that identifies individuals. This type of expression,

however, is quite complex and has not been studied in depth. Our limited sense of smell makes it difficult for us to understand this form of communication, but the olfactory sensitivity of wolves means they can perceive odors that are 'invisible' to us. Wolves urinate frequently to delimit their territory.

Whereas howling can be a sonic frontier, urine is its olfactory equivalent and proves effective in warning strangers off from the pack's territory. It also aids in allowing wolves to track one another down: if an individual leaves its territory for any reason, it can follow urine messages to find another pack. In other words, the messages represented by urine provide communication between wolves that are temporarily solitary (they are not solitary by nature) and other packs and allow them to behave accordingly.

Another much used form of communication between wolves is body language, which expresses emotions, mood and position within the clan. Each pack has a very varied set of postures that articulate information; the movements and position of a tail in particular provide very precise indications of the state and 'feelings' of an individual. For example, a wolf of modest rank in the hierarchy that timidly approaches another wolf will hold its tail down to indicate embarrassment as it does not know what reception it will be given.

When a wolf is afraid, it holds its tail between its back legs and flattens its ears. A friendly disposition is signaled by a relaxed tail that wags calmly. Threats are expressed by a tail held horizontally, with the ears and

hair on the back raised. Finally, if the tail is held horizontal but is slightly curved, the wolf is being provocative.

We know that a code of behavior exists between wolves and is applied by all. During a fight, the loser will demonstrate its submission by lying on its back and showing its belly and throat to its adversary. The winner will bare its fangs and content itself by threatening the loser for a few seconds, then, when the lesson has been clearly given, it will retire slowly, though still threateningly, with its tail held horizontal, feeling sure of itself, its own strength and the position or right it has acquired.

There are essentially two forms of behavior typical of dominance and submission but there are also intermediate ones that relate to the hierarchical position in the pack. The head plays the most important role in body language: the mouth open and fangs bared, the forehead furrowed, and the ears pointing slightly forward constitute a clear threat by a dominant wolf. Shyness, fear and uncertainty are expressed by a smooth forehead, closed mouth, and ears flattened and pointing backward. A wolf wishing to threaten and demonstrate self-assurance holds its tail high over its back while a submissive wolf will hold it between its legs.

When a dominant wolf decides to assert its rank inside the clan, submissive wolves assume a defensive or submissive posture, whether active or passive. An active posture of submission is offered when a wolf holds its body in a slightly hunched position, with the tail down and ears flat on its head; it may also lick or nibble the throat of the dominant animal and give out small whines. A passive posture is when the animal exposes its belly and genitals and holds its tail between its legs.

Observation of these forms of behavior and methods of communication have enabled great progress to be made in the understanding of these large canids. Their sonic and corporal languages are extremely complex so, with the constant desire to interpret them, it is easy to slip into equating them with their human equivalent. It should not be forgotten that each individual in a pack has its own character and personality, and that their relative positions may change rapidly.

Nothing remains the same, neither dominant nor submissive positions. Movement and behavior reveals a wolf's social position. Each individual has its own form of conduct that, in particular circumstances, is understood by the others, and a change of attitude can be sent by means of different postural messages or by sound.

The social life of wolves is well developed and important for the harmony of the pack; it follows from the fact that the individual members are able to express themselves with great articulateness. Whether they use sound, smell or body language, wolves can make contact with their fellow creatures in any circumstance. Such a highly developed ability constitutes a fundamental element of the social structure and permits harmonious relations between the members of a clan to be maintained.

A pack is reunited at the edge of the forest.
Inside the woods, each individual has a specific
role within a strictly maintained hierarchy.

126 bottom
The members of the group busy grooming,
cleaning each other's fur, in a sort of ritual that
can be interpreted both as a demonstration of
affection and as a way to honor a component of
the clan.

126-127
Open jaws baring gnashing teeth and a furrowed
brow are explicit signs of intimidation
given by an individual who is sure of itself
and its capabilities.

The wolf on the right has recognized its inferiority, giving a sign of submission by crouching down before the dominant animal, which looks down on it threateningly while other companions observe the scene.

Victory is complete: the animal on its feet, in a clear position of superiority, accepts the homage paid it by its adversary, which lies on its back exposing its genitals in confirmation of its unconditional surrender.

129

130-131

To foresee the outcome of this confrontation between two seasoned specimens, just observe the way in which they hold their ears: the wolf on the right, the most likely winner, keeps his ears pointed straight up with the hair on his head fluffed out; the other keeps his ears lowered, which does not bode well for him.

132

*During a fight, wolves always try to destabilize
their opponent, while keeping
their formidable claws well in sight.*

133

*The three photos clearly show the stages of
combat. The wolves confront each other, one of
them gets the better of the other, and then the
loser moves away with his tail between his legs.*

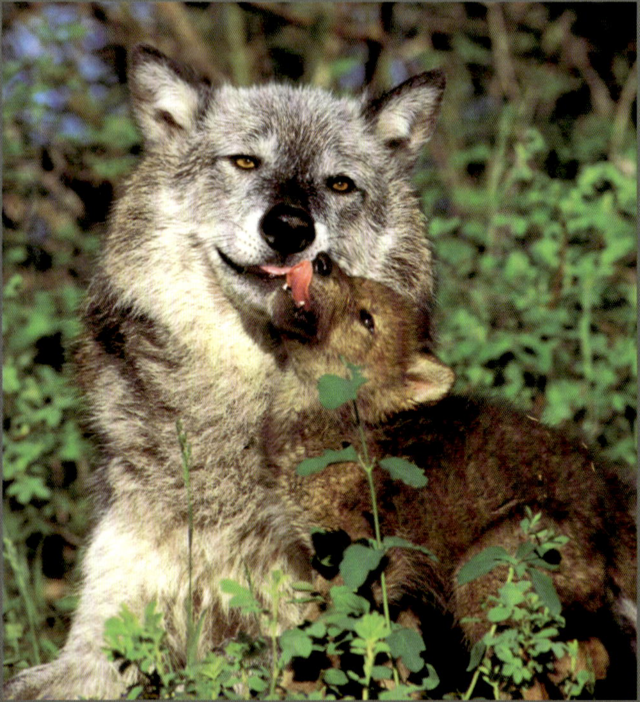
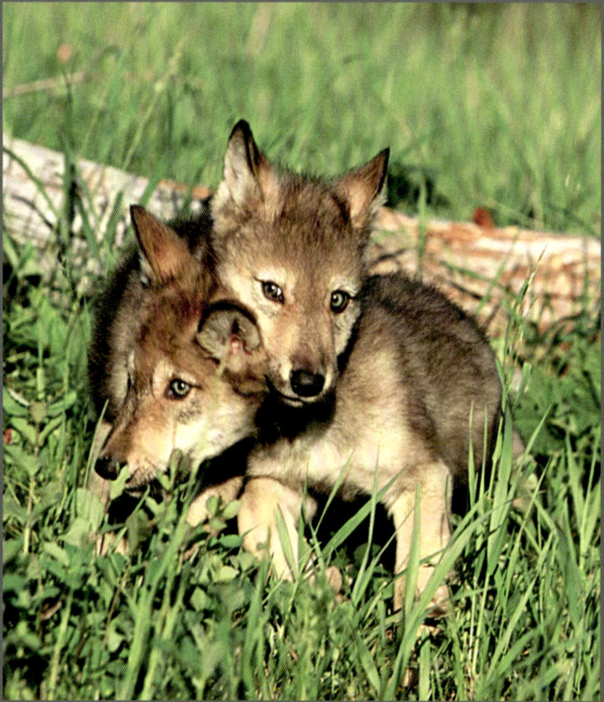

WOLF CUBS

134 left
Wolf cubs always have
very strong ties with
their parents, but also
with all the other members
of the pack.

134 right
Wolf cubs wait a few
weeks before taking their
first steps out of the den,
and then they never stray
too far.

136
At birth, wolf cubs are just
little balls of fur, blind and
totally vulnerable.

137
Wolf cubs only start to see
when about ten days old. It
will take time for them to
discover the immensity of
their territory.

Births occur in April and May in Europe and up until June in countries in which the winter is long and cold, for example, northern Canada. After two months gestation, on average between four and six cubs are born, though a first-time mother will have a smaller number of young.

A few days after the birth, the mother will prepare dens in different places so that if she feels danger threaten she can move her cubs; it is also an excellent method for evading the infestations of parasites that prosper in the dens.

The mother digs a very deep hole beneath a fallen tree or a bush; alternatively, she will use a cavity in a rock, a hollow tree or the den of another animal. She is a very fast digger with her front paws and, at times, uses her mouth. Dens and lairs are generally found close to water as the mother requires a large quantity of water during the suckling period. Being a prudent animal, the mother will also stash a quantity of meat near her refuge. I once saw a pregnant wolf urinate on a dozen or so pieces of meat, then bury them in different places in the Park; this was a wise precaution as just four days later she gave birth to seven cubs.

The cubs are born in spring so that they have time to grow and acquire strength before the rigors of winter set in. The cubs are born at irregular intervals that may last between five and sixty minutes. The mother frees them from their amniotic sac as soon as the cub is born, then bites the umbilical cord in two and eats it with the placenta. She licks the cubs all over, waits for them to dry, and delicately encircles them with her body to warm them.

Wolf cubs are born blind and deaf but they have excellent balance and their senses of touch and taste are already developed. After three or four days they begin to stumble around the den, moving extremely slowly and uncertainly. They return to their mother for milk, which they drink on average twelve times a day, and lie in a heap at her belly in search of warmth and her teats. In order for a cub to urinate, its mother has to massage its belly with her warm tongue to stimulate micturition; without help of this kind, small mammals are unable to urinate.

Around the tenth day of life, the cubs open their eyes and discover the world around them; they begin to explore and growl. Five days later, with the appearance of their first teeth, they begin to chew.

Not all cubs survive and it is not rare that one or two will die young. In this case the mother will keep the tiny body inside the den for a couple of days, then, when she understands there is nothing she can do, she carries it outside and, in about half the cases, she will bury it. We should not, however, consider this a funerary ritual, but rather the instinct to bury meat that might later be required to feed herself or another member of the clan. In some circumstances the mother will put an end to the suffering of a cub that is too delicate to survive, but female wolves are excellent parents and take care of their offspring with great devotion.

138
At two months old, the wolf cub starts to wander around a bit, but its parents watch him closely.

139
When the adults carry their cubs, they never grab them by the neck but by the skin on their back, holding them between their jaws.

The cubs are suckled for about six weeks, during which time the mother protects them jealously from the attentions of other females, which can sometimes be too close.

Weaning is rapid: the first teeth grow, the milk dries up and at times the mother will move away from her cubs rather suddenly if they are overly insistent. This is the period in which the mother, though continuing to watch over her young, demands help from other females in the pack who are willing to act as wet-nurses.

Remaining close to the den, the male and other members of the clan keep a watchful eye out. The whole group is very involved in the birth of the young and each animal takes pains to make its own contribution.

In Gévaudan Park, where I have observed the lives of wolves for several years, I have seen a male spend many hours close to the den, one spring after another, waiting for the first cub to come out. After three weeks, when one more courageous than his siblings made his appearance, the male took the cub delicately in his mouth and carried him proudly around for a few minutes before crouching and placing him carefully between his paws. I noted the tenderness with which he regarded and licked the cub. At that moment the mother arrived to take her youngster back but that did not stop the male from repeating the operation several times a day. Adult wolves are endlessly patient with cubs. All members of the pack 'worry' for their well-being and are often remarkably 'maternal' in their behavior.

Cubs keep their milk teeth until the age of four months, when their final set of teeth appears. However, their mothers offer them meat to eat as early as their third or fourth week. All members of the pack contribute to feeding the young. When a cub is hungry, it will call to an adult, whether its mother or not, and gnaw its lips; the adult wolf will then regurgitate part of the food it has eaten and offer it to the cub. Regurgitation (also used by birds) consists of returning the contents of the stomach or esophagus to the mouth; it is a form of voluntary vomit used to nourish the new generation.

As soon as the cubs leave the den for the first time (around the age of three weeks), they explore their new environment but only under the strict surveillance of the adults. The cubs are the main preoccupation of the whole pack, both young and old, who help feed them, surround them with attention and contribute to their education. After all, cubs are of major importance to the survival of the group and, in consequence, of the entire species.

Between the ages of three and ten weeks, more or less, there is a rapid development of social behavior. The cubs play, provoke one another, and fight, thus learning both to dominate and submit and to use the different types of social behavior that govern the life of the pack. The hierarchy that exists between the adults also takes form amongst the cubs. Occasionally the games degenerate into a brawl, which helps to create this hierarchy, and a more daring, stronger or perhaps more aggressive cub may develop into the dominant member of the litter.

This does not mean that the position it wins as a cub will extend into adulthood, as many events may occur up till the age of maturity that could turn a 'baby leader' into a submissive adult.

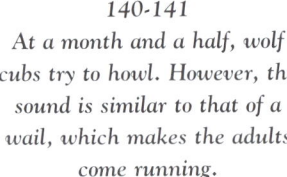

140-141
At a month and a half, wolf cubs try to howl. However, the sound is similar to that of a wail, which makes the adults come running.

When we are fortunate enough to observe a pack for many years consecutively, dramatic changes in behavior, attitude and even character become apparent. Depending on the context, the position of a wolf in a pack can change radically, either positively or negatively: nothing is ever definitive.

From the age of two months, following the example of the adults, the young begin to howl, run, jump, climb and play. For the first five or six months of life, they enjoy every kind of privilege, and I have even seen cubs take meat out of the mouths of the adults without any kind of reaction or disapproval being shown; however, after this period their education becomes more exacting.

Wolves are always extremely patient with cubs. If an adult is woken unexpectedly by an assault of cubs, then it will stand up and go and move away, and if the cubs are insistent, it will simply wander further off, but without snarling or showing any sign of aggressiveness. On occasion, adults will join in the cubs' games, run with them, follow them, hide and jump on them, nipping them playfully but careful never to hurt.

The atmosphere in the pack is joyful and almost light-hearted. Their games are fun-filled and, though they last just a few minutes, they may be repeated several times during a day. Even the older wolves join in these happy interludes, seeming to be invested with a burst of youthfulness and exuberance. These are intense moments in which everyone forgets the difficulties of life in a somewhat inhospitable environment, and the tensions that inevitably arise in a pack.

142
The parents spend a lot of time with their little ones, strengthening family ties and stimulating learning.

143
Wolf cubs are unable to hunt. Fed by the pack, every now and then they enjoy showing off their trophies.

144-145
A field of dandelions can make for a wonderful playground for a wolf cub on his first day out.

For the cubs the games result in a great expenditure of energy, so there are long rest periods in the shelter of bushes, beneath trees or just curled up close to their mothers. It is rare that the cubs return to the den to sleep unless they hear an unusual sound or there is danger at hand, something they learn from the tension existing between the adults. The cubs quickly pick up on the restlessness of the mature wolves, and rapidly learn to be cautious in their behavior in spite of the constant presence of the pack. When there are cubs in the pack, all the adults' attention is focused on them, particularly that of the females who have not acquired a high social position. They devote themselves to the cubs, thereby succeeding in playing an important role in the clan. I have seen a gentle but insecure female wolf in Canada become more self-assured with the arrival of cubs. She quickly took on the role of wet-nurse with dedication and was the first to protect the cubs at the slightest hint of danger. She remained alert, with her fur raised on her back and her slightly wavy tail held horizontal. She had found her place in the pack and her behavior was in consequence greatly changed. The role of the adults is decisive in the development of the cubs, yet despite the constant protection and affectionate care lavished on them, about 60% of cubs do not reach adulthood. Their selection is the result of external factors, such as difficulty in procuring food, or weather conditions and sickness.

Within the same litter, not all the cubs develop at the same rate and their individual weights may vary significantly, even between members of the same sex, particularly when growth is very rapid. A cub's skeleton continues to grow for at least eighteen months while muscular and sexual development last until maturity is reached at the age of three years. The disparity in size between youngsters of different sex is very evident, with the females being smaller, lighter and having a more slender muzzle.

Wolves have an innate hunting instinct but they have no aptitude for killing. This large canid is a predator but kills only to feed. For cubs, hunting starts as a game and, when just a month old, they are able to capture their first prey. I have seen a five-week-old cub throw itself at the throat of a passing vole. He bit it and then, disturbed by 'this living thing,' let it go. The vole, somewhat upset, tried to make off but at that moment the 'game' got interesting and the cub began to strike it with its paws; he then grabbed hold of the vole again and gobbled it down. Proud of his achievement, the cub lay down and licked his whiskers like a real gourmet.

The cub had passed the first important test of his young life. At five or six months, the young are big enough to follow adults during a hunt. Assiduously imitating the pack's behavior and following its tactics, the cubs learn what will be indispensable to them in adult life. To tackle larger prey, the young need the support of older pack members because, despite their energy and vitality, they lack the experience and strength of an adult.

The life of the pack is organized around the needs and education of the young. Their constant care and attention are the result of a complex social organization that permits the species to continue in the best manner possible. When the cubs' infancy is past, the educational methods become more stringent: this is the phase of apprenticeship for adulthood, with its laws and regulations. The time of a carefree existence is over, at the age of six months the cub has grown into a young wolf.

When cubs nibble the lips of the adults they are
actually facilitating the process of regurgitation,
they way in which they are fed once they are
weaned.

This Montana female would enjoy a bit of a rest,
but her cub would prefer to cuddle or play.

148
Wolf cubs learn about life by always being
among adults.

149
Female wolves are truly excellent mothers.
Nevertheless, male wolves are also model
fathers, devoted to and patient with their little
ones.

150
A mother with her cubs: among northern wolves, if one parents is black and one is white, the little ones can turn out randomly to be either of the colors.

150-151
The wolf cubs cluster at their mother's muzzle. She has apparently returned from the hunt and is hurrying to regurgitate part of what she has swallowed.

152-153
At the first sign of trouble, the little ones take refuge in their den. If the den is too far, they hide between the paws of the adults in the pack.

154
The carefree attitude of childhood, common to cubs of every species, makes wolf cubs extremely playful.

154-155
A six-week-old wolf cub takes a few moments to rest. At this age, and for some time to come, the little creature is extremely vulnerable.

156-157
An adult male gives a year-old cub a series of warnings. The position of their tails can be noticed: the cub submissive, the adult dominant.

158
Taking its first steps, a cub may be a bit afraid to get wet and prefer to lean on a reassuring shoulder.

159
The wolf always pays attention to the needs of its little ones. If they get too excited, the adult may distance itself a few feet ... but it is almost always caught up with.

Around a month and a half to two years old, the cubs can follow the adults on their walks, but they still cannot participate in the hunt.

161

Discovering new territory is done step by step and always under the watch of the adults. A little bit at a time, the wolf cub gets to know his environment, above all through smell.

162-163
*Cubs are spoiled and cuddled until they are
about five or six months old. Then, they enter a
more difficult phase in which they are educated
on severe principles and with great strictness.*

164

In some way, howling also expresses a sense of belonging to the group. It is never too late to get on the pack's good side....

165

For wolf cubs, everything that surrounds them is an excuse to play, be it a butterfly or, in this case, a blade of grass.

166-167

Young wolves in North America: though they are already very strong, they would surely have difficulty surviving on their own.

168-169
Scuffles among brothers and sisters never get out of hand. They actually help the siblings to strengthen their relationships.

169
At two months old, the wolf cubs are already simulating real combat in their playing. It could be useful.

170
Anything is good for sharpening teeth (even baby teeth). In this case, the object is a deer antler, just hard enough.

171
This wolf cub, which watches over his brothers and sisters, is already showing a dominant attitude with his tail proudly held high.

172-173
Wolf cubs near their den, in Alaska: dens can be very deep or, at times, reduced to the bare minimum. It depends on the circumstances.

174
Idaho: two wolf cubs frisk around together. This is the age of exploration and their worries are still but few.

175
A wolf cub knows how to be gentle, with its pointed ears and chubby body, but it also knows how to show off its agility and, sometimes, even seems to concentrate.

Hunting and Prey

WOLVES HUNTING AND PREY

PREY

AND

HUNTING

WOLVES

178

176 left
A fawn has fell victim to the pack, which hunts closely together before dividing up their communal booty.

176 right
This specimen gnashes its teeth in a threatening way to discourage any potential competitors from considering stealing its prey.

178
During winter, wolves appear in all their glory thanks to the presence of a thick layer of downy fluff under their fur.

179
During meals, wolves often change their attitude. Each must guard its own morsel.

HUNTING AND PREY

Wolves are predators in the literal sense of the word: they kill only to feed, choosing their prey according to the season and biotope.

This large canid knows how to economize its energy. It does not create complications for itself and as willingly hunts small animals like muskrats, rabbits and hares as large prey like caribou and moose. When attacking large animals, wolves act together in a hierarchical pack. Competition for prey is strong as other predators – man, bears, pumas, lynxes, coyotes, wolverines and foxes – threaten their hunting grounds.

Wolves are equipped with long, slender legs and a broad chest; they have enormous stamina and are perfectly adapted for the long-distance chase. Their principal qualities as hunters are their endurance and intelligence, but they also have acute hearing and an extremely sensitive sense of smell that allows them to register the presence of prey at a distance of a mile and a half.

The first phase of the hunt is represented by observation. They are opportunist creatures and are able to detect sick, young or wounded animals that will offer little resistance; they will then surround and attack the most vulnerable.

Smell plays a fundamental role in localizing the victim but the encounter may also happen by chance, an occurrence that is more probable in territories where the density of prey is high.

Rarely is the hunted animal killed at once. First the pack tries to prevent the quarry's escape by biting its feet, back and flanks, and often more than one attack and a long chase is required before it succumbs.

Wolves nearly always devour their prey immediately, at least in part. When food is abundant, they will eat only the most nourishing part of the animal so that they receive the maximum quantity of energy in the minimum time. Wolves never kill more than is necessary for their well-being and they know how to organize themselves to gain that end. When hunting large prey they are obliged to act together but even in this case only one attempt in ten will end in success. If, for example, an adult caribou fights, it stands a good chance of escape. On Isle Royale, off Lake Superior's northern shore, David Mech noted that in 100 attacks by wolves on adult moose, only 6 were killed, 58 succeeded in escaping, and 36 successfully fought their aggressors. In winter wolves eat hoofed mammals like moose, caribou, musk-ox and roe deer, prey which are hunted by the pack. When individuals in the same pack work together, the chances of success are increased. When the prey is killed, each member of the group has the right to eat, but in strict hierarchical order. In summer, when wolves hunt separately for themselves, they eat smaller animals – generally rodents, marmots, rabbits, etc. Whether they hunt together or separately depends on the season and the size of the prey. Some wolves prefer to hunt alone and organize themselves better that way. An example might be when their teeth are worn, which prevents them from participating successfully in a pack hunt.

Another hunting skill wolves have is their ability to fish in shallow water, but, being intelligent creatures, they also exploit the victims of other predators.

In winter, wolves capture larger prey that get stuck in the snow because of their greater weight.

181
Prey like the deer in the photograph can keep the whole pack fed and happy for several days, whether here in the Rocky Mountains or elsewhere.

For instance, in Alaska wolves have been seen watching grizzlies hunting salmon. It is typical behavior of these bears to kill more than they need to eat, and the wolves take advantage of this by feeding on the leftovers.

Wolves will occasionally eat from carcasses as their digestive juices allow them to assimilate meat in an advanced state of putrefaction. Over the entire year, animal carcasses represent 15–20% of their food intake and are eaten in all seasons.

When a large animal is killed, such as a moose which can weigh from 900 to 1,300 lbs, or a wapiti (650–900 lbs), the wolves will not eat it all even if the pack numbers fifteen or so. During the summer, if they kill a large animal they will only eat their fill, then leave the rest to the foxes, wolverines, birds of prey and crows. In winter, though, once they are replete, they will remain near the carcass to keep other predators away until they have completely finished it.

In America's northern-tier state of Minnesota, where several hundreds of wolves live, the zoologist G. E. Johnson has seen a wolf eat the floating carcass of a moose. It moved in the water as it tore the flesh. It is not rare for these large reindeer to try to escape from a pack by entering deep water. This is a good refuge as the wolves, forced to swim, lose the coordination of their attack and moose are good swimmers. In water over three feet deep, the moose stands a good chance of getting away.

After a long chase, whether it has been successful or not, rest is essential and the wolves will sleep for several hours.

However, they are capable of recovering their strength quickly and this is a fundamental benefit as hunts are not always productive.

Large prey is mostly hunted in winter when the snow almost always favors the wolves. Let's take the example of a herd chasing an adult moose, whose weight can reach 1,300 lbs and as much as 1,750 among the giants in Alaska and northern Siberia. If the snow is fresh and thick, the wolves do not receive much benefit as they sink in the snow, whereas the moose, thanks to its extremely long legs, can outrun its followers. But when the snow is hard as a result of low temperatures, the wolves are greatly advantaged as the pressure of their paws on the ground averages 22.4 lbs per square inch compared to the 68.2 of the moose.

Moose have a fairly effective response by gathering in the conifer forests, but this type of defense causes lacks in their food intake that make the young in particular more vulnerable to the wolves.

However, moose are difficult to bring down in any case. David Mech described a hunt that ended in failure. "On Isle Royale in February 1954, fifteen or so wolves were walking in single file by the shore of Lake Sikiwit. Suddenly they stopped: they had seen three moose trotting ahead. Still in a line, the wolves began to follow them for about 250 yards. When the wolves were about 30 yards away, two of the moose realized they were being followed and accelerated. The third, however, was immediately circled. It tried to escape but without success. Five wolves attacked, biting its rear legs and flanks.

182-183
Alaska, Denali National Park:
a caribou faces off against a
wolf. If other wolves do not
come to help it quickly, the
caribou could get away.

The moose continued to run dragging its assailants with it. It fell to the ground but managed to get to its feet, then it fell again and another wolf attached itself to the moose's nose. It struggled once more to its feet and succeeded in reaching a copse. A moment later and the five wolves surrounded it but the moose defended itself vigorously with its horns. A day later the moose was still alive and the wolves had disappeared."

In Lapland reindeer are the wolves' favorite prey, a fact that the reindeer herders, the Sami, dislike. Even a caribou just three weeks old is able to run faster than a wolf, and this explains why wolves rarely follow one in good health. When they force a herd of reindeer to run away from them, the purpose of the wolves is to assess the health of its members as the group may include sick or injured animals that the wolves can concentrate on. If they decide to attack a large animal, like a cow, horse or moose, they nearly always try to break the tendons on the creature's rear legs, but when they attack a caribou, which weighs even more than a moose, they attack its shoulders or neck directly. The reason for this is that the wolves are afraid of the caribou's kicks because its sharp hooves could seriously injure them.

Wolves rarely attack bison but when the climate is particularly cold many bison get sick with tuberculosis, brucellosis, or arthritis, and become the designated victims. A pack of a dozen wolves is able to bring a sick, old or weakened bison down.

In Poland, European bison are often the victims of wolves. An episode that took place in Plex Park is reported in which a two-year-old female was attacked and torn to pieces.

184
This powerful hunter also knows how to take advantage of prey less challenging than elk and caribou. Small-size animals constitute an important part of wolves' diets.

185
Although winter is the best time for tracking large prey, in this season wolves do not disdain either rodents or other small inhabitants of their ecosystem.

The musk-ox is also a potential prey but difficult to catch as it understands the danger posed by wolves. If a lone wolf approaches a group of musk-oxen, the latter stop and watch until the threat retreats, then they continue to graze. Wolves fear musk-oxen because an adult male can weigh up to 1,300 lbs and, despite its ungainly appearance, it is an exceptionally agile animal. Results in the field reflect the animals' relative values: out of 26 observed attacks, only 3 were successful.

Deer also form a part of wolves' diet. I once saw an adult deer killed by two wolves, but it only went down after fighting strenuously and gravely injuring one of its attackers with its horns. Deer (usually roe deer) are a favorite target in much of central Europe. The wolf is a predator, one of the best in the animal world, and the most successful (excepting man) in the Palearctic and Nearctic (in bio-geography the Palearctic refers to the areas of Europe, non-tropical Asia and northern Africa, while the Nearctic covers North America down to Mexico).

A wolf's diet is varied. From time to time it will attack domesticated animals and, as is well known, it favors sheep, though dogs are a more fearsome enemy for sheep than wolves. Every year in France herds of sheep suffer heavy losses from dogs. To know the extent of the damage, ask the sheep-farmers or consult the petitions drawn up to try to prevent the slaughter. Wild dogs are capable of massacring dozens of sheep in just a few minutes because they get excited, something that never happens to a wolf. After killing a lamb, a wolf would not attack others simply for enjoyment, however, wolves make the perfect scapegoat for dog attacks in regions where wolves have made their reappearance.

Sometimes a wolf will kill a cow; it circles the cow,

avoiding swipes of the horns but as the cow tires, so its defense becomes less accurate. When it attacks, the wolf will try to sever the cow's rear tendons so that it is at its mercy. However, when domesticated animals are watched over by man, wolves will not approach and will look for other prey. Other creatures that make up a wolf's diet are rats, mice, water voles and lemmings. It is even willing to try its paw at fishing or catching frogs and birds, for example, ptarmigans and black partridges.

Being opportunists, they will ally themselves with other animals – all living beings are interdependent. Wolves will follow the flight of crows to find a carcass, but the opposite also occurs as crows will monitor the movements of wolves and, after a kill, when the wolves move off, will swoop down on the remains.

This sort of collaboration between very different species contributes to maintaining the balance of nature. Each creature has its own role and place in the order of things.

Hunting is an activity in which the entire pack participates except for females that have recently given birth. For a certain period, a mother will remain next to her young in the den allowing males and other females to bring them food. The mother will only return to the hunt when the cubs are older and larger.

In winter the cubs are old enough to follow the adults but they must be pretty strong to keep up when large animals are being hunted. If the snow is deep or the chase long, not all the young will pass the test. The weaker members will fall behind while the others will learn to hunt large prey together with the adults.

The path to become an adult wolf is a hard one. Life in the wild revolves around the hunt, and is regulated by hunger and the struggle for survival. Wolves never kill pointlessly.

186-187
Wolves do not scorn small prey: it represents a good source of energy, especially when there are little ones to feed.

187
If the prey is too bulky, it will not be carried off. Rather, the whole pack will travel to it.

188-189
But a fleeting glimpse and always silent: a wolf has passed by. Was it really a wolf or was it a dream? Let it hunt in peace.

190 and 191
Grizzly bears can fight with wolves, perhaps because they happen to end up too close to each other or because they are hunting the same prey. It is not always the wolves to have to leave the scene.

192 and 193
Dividing up a catch always lets loose some nasty outbursts – and some teeth snapping – in all species. It is not real aggressiveness; it is just part of the ritual, and everybody gets their bit in the end.

194-195
Two specimens of the timber wolf (canis lupus lycaon), a subspecies of the gray wolf found in the United States and parts of Canada, clean off the bones of an animal that they have caught and killed.

196-197
*In winter, prey is less abundant, and wolves
may travel far from their dens in tracking
their victims.*

198-199
A wolf defends its catch: the indecision between an openly hostile attitude, considering its superiority, and a more apprehensive behavior can be noted.

199
The male normally serves himself before the female. However, it may be that he has to demand respect in a more dramatic way.

200-201
Smaller-size prey that can be easily carried will be devoured quickly.

201
For wolf cubs around just two months old, a hare is perfect, both for its protein content and for getting used to digesting meat.

202
A genet has just ended up in the teeth of this hungry young wolf. It will not be a very abundant meal.

203
Thanks to the extraordinary strength of its neck muscles, a wolf in its prime is able to drag a wild boar without any trouble, simply grabbing it firmly by the throat.

204
*In Alaska, and more precisely in Denali
National Park, wolves can live in peace without
fear of being disturbed by man.*

205
*Sometimes the coat of the wolf has a reddish
color, like this specimen, which is trying hard to
hide itself among the tall grasses.*

Wolves are very good at flushing small prey out of their holes hidden under the snow. In these instances, the senses of hearing and smell must come into play simultaneously.

Weaker, sicker, or older animals – or even, as in this case, newborns – are easy prey for wolves that generally look for the easiest solution to hunger.

208

This large wolf in Alaska makes it clear that it does not appreciate anyone going near his prey. Teeth bared and ears lowered indicate that it does not intend to joke around anymore.

208-209

Sometimes the dominant male has some trouble enforcing the rules of good manners in the division of a large catch. It tries its best, even if some others cheat by snatching morsels.

210-211

A face-off, on a river bank in Alaska, between a wolf and a bear over an elk carcass: the wolf appears to cautiously make do with a salmon.

212-213

Wolves can even compete with pumas for prey. Often, as in this case in Montana, each goes for a different portion, thus avoiding direct confrontation, which would be dangerous for both.

208

213

This large gray wolf protects its catch with very typical behavior.

214 and 215

A small rodent running over the snow has little to no chance of escaping a hungry wolf, or one that simply feels like having a little fun. In some regions, and in specific periods of the year, the wolf feeds almost exclusively on small prey.

216-217
Birch trees, the snow, a wolf proceeding warily:
a picture-perfect scene from the Great North.

218-219
Wolves can hunt in packs and on open land, but
they can also approach their prey slowly through
woodland, proof of their cleverness and ability to
be silent.

220
Two wolves run free in the snow on the plains at
the foot of the Rocky Mountains.

A U T H O R S

Anne Dominique Ménatory was born in Alès (Gard) in 1958. Her father was the legendary Gérard Ménatory, environmentalist and naturalist of worldwide renown and founder of Gévaudan Park, an animal reserve in the Massif Central region of France, created in 1985 for the study and protection of wolves. Gérard Ménatory dedicated about 40 years of his life to studying canis lupus, following the species at every latitude, in semi-freedom, within vast fenced-in areas, until he completed his series of experiments with the so-called "imprinting" learning process on the wolf cub. Even though personal enthusiasms are not genetically inherited, Anne Dominique's interest in wolves is without doubt the result of her father's influence, with whom she worked side by side in his research and administration of the nature reserve for many years. Upon Gérard's death in 1998, Anne Dominique took over running the park, thus carrying on her illustrious father's work and fighting for the survival of one of the most highly endangered species in Europe. She has participated in numerous conferences dealing with environmental issues and has dedicated some of her works to other canine species, such as the African hunting dog, which she has studied during her travels in East Africa. She has collaborated with the Museum of Natural History in Paris and with famous documentary directors like Bruno Vienne, with whom she made the feature film Brother Wolf, distributed by National Geographic throughout the world. She has also worked with a variety of environmental organizations and many specialized magazines.

Gianni Guadalupi was born in 1943 and worked in the publishing for 30 years as a writer, translator and compiler of anthologies, concentrating in particular on literature pertaining to travel, both real and imaginary. He has been editor of *FMR* and associate editor of *Le Vie del Mondo*, the magazine dedicated to travels of yesteryear published by the Touring Club of Italy, as well as editor of the series entitled *Guide Impossibili*, *Antichi Stati* and *Grand Tour*, published by Franco Maria Ricci. He is the author of *Dictionary of Imaginary Places* (with Alberto Manguel). Guadalupi has written numerous successful books dedicated to the culture of travel; his topics include the Jesuits in China; travels in 18th-century Persia; space travel; the Portuguese in India; 18th-century travelers to the Orient; the discovery of America; and Italian aeronautical pioneers. For White Star Publishers he has written *The Discovery of the Nile* (1997), *The Great Treasures. The Goldsmith's Art from Ancient Egypt to the 20th Century* (1998), *China Revealed* (2003), *The Holy Bible* (2003), and the historical chapters of *Marco Polo* (2002), *Sahara* (2003), *China. The Kingdom of the Dragon* (2005), *Zheng He: Tracing the Epic Voyages of China's Greatest Explorer* (2006), as well as the historical chapters of books belonging to the series entitled *The Art of Being...*

P H O T O G R A P H I C   C R E D I T S

Cover

Howling is more than just a call: it is one of the forms of communication within the pack and one of the wolf's distinctive traits. © R. Wittek/ Blickwinkel

Back cover

Golden eyes and an intelligent but ruthless expression: the wolf's gaze is that of one of the most fearsome predators in existence. © Mary Clay/ Ardea